Buy,
Rent,
&
Hold

Other McGraw-Hill Books by Robert Irwin

The McGraw-Hill Real Estate Handbook (1984)

The Handbook of Property Management (1986)

Making Mortgages Work For You (1987)

Tips and Traps When Buying a Home (1990)

Tips and Traps When Selling a Home (1990)

How to Find Hidden Real Estate Bargains, Second Edition (1991)

Buy, Rent, & Hold

How to Make Money in a "Cold" Real Estate Market

Robert Irwin

McGraw-Hill, Inc.

New York St. Louis San Francisco Auckland Bogotá
Caracas Lisbon London Madrid Mexico Milan
Montreal New Delhi Paris San Juan São Paulo
Singapore Sydney Tokyo Toronto

Library of Congress Cataloging-in-Publication Data
Irwin, Robert
  Buy, rent, & hold: how to make money in a "cold" real estate
market / Robert Irwin.
    p.   cm.
  Includes index.
  ISBN 0-07-032236-8.—ISBN 0-07-032235-X (pbk.)
  1. Real estate investment. 2. Real estate business. I. Title.
II. Title: Buy, rent, and hold.
  HD1382.5.I69 1991
  332.63'24—dc20   91-7996
                                                                CIP

    3 4 5 6 7 8 9 0   DOC/DOC 9 6 5 4 3

ISBN 0-07-032235-X {PBK}
ISBN 0-07-032236-8 {HC}

*The sponsoring editor for this book was James Bessent, the editing supervisor
was Jim Halston, and the production supervisor was Suzanne W. Babeuf.
This book was set in Baskerville by Carol Woolverton, Lexington, Mass.*

Printed and bound by R. R. Donnelley and Sons

Contents

Preface

The people at McGraw-Hill came to me and suggested that it might be a good time to write a book about investing in real estate. The country was in the grips of the deepest recession since the Great Depression. Real estate prices were off. And as a consequence, for those with the gumption to take a risk, there appeared to be plenty of opportunities. I, being a real estate investor, agreed.

No, this wasn't last month or even last year. It was 1973. The book that was written was called *How to Buy and Sell Real Estate For Financial Security.*

Needless to say it sold very well and launched many people into personal investing in real estate. Those who got in were in the perfect position to take advantage of the biggest run up in real estate prices in this century, which happened in the late 1970s. They profited enormously.

The question today, of course, is whether or not history may be repeating itself?

There are striking parallels, just as there are dissimilarities between now and the recession of 1973–1974. But what is certain is that in most areas of the country, the price of real estate is falling. Values are dropping by ten, twenty, in some cases, thirty percent! That everyone knows.

I personally believe that they will not fall forever. Further, I believe they will level off sooner than later. And finally, I think that no later than the middle of this decade, we are going to be back in an inflationary economy that will send prices soaring once again.

Therefore, when McGraw-Hill again suggested a similar book, only one geared specifically to this market, I didn't hesitate a moment. *Buy, Rent, & Hold* is the result.

This book gives you my most conservative approach to profiting from the current real estate slump. In it I give a strategy for obtaining houses, for renting them out to make your payments, and for holding onto them until the market turns around and you can sell for a big profit.

You know, it doesn't take a great deal of savvy to make money in real estate. It's simple, like anything else—you buy low and sell high.

What it does take is the ability to remember that some day the market will, indeed, turn around; the courage to move forward when everyone else is preaching doom and gloom, which is the best time to buy; and the fortitude to hang on during the tough years.

In this book I don't want to sell you on doing anything. I do, however, want to present you with some investment options to consider. Most important, I want to give you the chance never again to have to say, "If only I had bought back when . . ."

Robert Irwin

Buy,
Rent,
&
Hold

Introduction

Let's start with a tip right off the bat . . .

Tip

Don't listen to the pessimists.

I was recently talking with a very successful professional about his investments. He had dabbled in stocks, commodities, bonds, raising avocados, and growing grapes for wine. After a pause in the conversation, he looked thoughtful and said, "You know, thinking back, about the only place that I've ever made any real money is in real estate."

His comments have been echoed by literally millions of Americans, most of them middle-class people, who have had the same result. They've tried a lot of other investments, often pushed by stock-, insurance-, and commodity brokers eager to make commissions. And while they may have broken even or gotten a reasonable return on these investments, about the only place that they've really done well in a big way is in real estate, typically on the sales of their houses. It's no surprise, therefore, that real estate has been termed "the last great hope of the small investor in America."

Yet today, all of that seems to be changing. For the first time in most people's memories, real estate appears to be in trouble. From one coast to the other the price of homes (and condos and co-ops) is going down instead of up. Could it be, many are wondering, that the great real estate bonanza of the last 50 years has finally drawn to a close? The statistics are disheartening.

New York. The number of single-family houses sold statewide (including condos and co-ops) in 1987 totaled 223,900. In 1988 it was 213,400. In 1989 it was 187,400 and the downward trend seems to continue.

Los Angeles. In April of 1989 the San Fernando Valley (the big bedroom community for Los Angeles) had over 11,000 homes in unsold inventory, one of the highest levels it had ever recorded.

Florida and parts of the south. The number of condos for sale and remaining unsold for more than 6 months has doubled in Florida. In other parts of the south houses go begging for buyers.

Southwest, particularly Arizona. A rapid decline began in 1987. In Arizona prices in some areas have tumbled by more than 50 percent. Scandals in the savings and loan industry have led to large-scale dumping of homes.

Oil patch states. Texas and Oklahoma are particularly hard hit. The Resolution Trust Corporation (RTC) set up to handle insolvent savings and loans has more foreclosed property in Texas than in almost all the rest of the United States combined.

Midwest. Depressed prices in agriculture have resulted in declining real estate values since the early 1980s. With only a partial recovery there, prices in many areas are still 40 percent below their all time highs.

West Coast. Once considered the top real estate market in the country, layoffs in aerospace, defense, and electronics (from the easing of tensions between the Soviet Union and the United States) have resulted in a recessionary economy. In Los Angeles prices have fallen 15 to 20 percent. In California's central valley, once immune to real estate problems, the inventory of unsold houses is skyrocketing. Even in San Francisco, oftentimes the highest-priced real estate market in the country, sales are lagging.

With real estate *losing* value in 85 percent of the country for perhaps the first time since the Second World War, many people are backing away. They are saying that homes are no longer the best place to put your money, that buying investment property doesn't make sense, that there really is no longer any place the average person can make a big profit in a relatively short time with a minimum investment.

This book will show you that such doomsayers are wrong. In my opinion, now is not the worst time to invest in real estate, it's the best. Rather than the spigot being turned off on home investment properties, it's being turned on. Real estate investing in the United States is getting ready for the biggest price explosion in history and those who don't have the foresight to see what's really happening will lose out.

Foreign Investment

Unfortunately, those who are going to lose out will mostly be middle-class Americans, small investors, those who should be reaping the rewards. And many of those who will probably be the big winners are foreigners, wealthy foreigners. It's a fact that every year of the 1980s and particularly during the last few years when prices declined, foreign investment has increased in the United States. The heaviest investors include the British buying corporations and large properties. The Dutch, Japanese, French, Germans, and other foreign investors are right behind buying a variety of real estate.

A great deal of foreign buying has actually been directed at single-family rental houses, typically the higher-priced homes. (I have a real estate broker friend in Los Angeles who has become a multimillionaire in the last 2 years simply by selling expensive rental investment homes to Asian investors. And they all pay cash.)

Ever since the French writer Alexis de Tocqueville wrote his remarkable essay in the last century analyzing American culture, it's become a truism that a visitor can often see more clearly what's happening in a community than someone who lives there. This is apparently the case with foreign investors who see the recently falling prices of American real estate as wonderful buying opportunities. While we Americans worry about budget deficits and recession, foreigners see a stable government and housing shortages. While we worry about high prices, foreigners see an incipient inflation that makes today's prices low by comparison with anticipated future prices. While we worry that the housing market has collapsed, foreigners see the cyclical nature of housing and realize that today's lows are just the foundation for tomorrow's highs. While we worry about losing our money when we invest 10 percent down in a house, foreigners gladly put in 100 percent on what they see as a sure thing. While we Americans are bearish, foreigners are bullish on housing.

If you want to avoid being the next big loser in the real estate market, you need to see things differently. You need to see the housing market in this country through the eyes of those outside. Only then will you realize its true potential.

In This Book

What you'll discover in this book is that housing hasn't abandoned the small investor. It's the small investor who has wavered. Many of those who could be setting the stage right now for big profits are losing out. On the other hand, those who will profit immensely are the small investors with the foresight to realize that beyond each housing market decline is a new housing market boom.

In this book you'll be given techniques that will allow you to gauge the depth of the market's decline, to see when it's reached bottom. Thus, you'll be able to tell just when to buy to avoid losing money on your purchase.

You'll then learn how to buy properties at distressed prices. You won't pay what the seller is asking. You'll pay much less. You'll also be able to buy at auction, from the government, and through foreclosure.

Finally, you'll see how to rent property for most of your costs. Thus, you'll be able to rent and hold through the relatively short time it takes for the turnaround to occur. Finally, you'll learn how to reap profits from refinancing and selling.

This book will give you the information you need to profit from the current real estate recession.

1
The Opportunity of a Lifetime

In ancient Greece, the philosopher Parmenides was criticized for his poverty. Young men of his time said, "Why should we listen to your words, when your wisdom is not great enough to bring food to your table nor a home to shelter you from the rain?"

Some philosophers might have had a ready retort such as Wisdom is food for the mind and shelter for the heart. But Parmenides was of a more practical nature. He listened to what was said and decided that in order to influence the minds of others, he must set an example.

So he gazed at the stars and made a decision. Borrowing money from friends, he bought up all the olive presses in the city and surrounding areas and then waited. That summer was a bumper year for olives and the farmers needed the olive presses. Parmenides provided them, for a high price. From that one season, Parmenides retired wealthy, and the young men flocked to him for his "valuable" advice.

The question he was most often asked was, "How did you make so much money so fast?" Parmenides would smile and then say those four words which echo down through the millennia to us today, "Buy low, sell high!"

Easy to Say, Difficult to Apply

Simple? Even simple-minded? Maybe. But those four words are the key to investment success in any commodity and that includes real estate. The real trick, of course, is having the courage to follow through.

When prices are going up, it's very easy to say, "Now's the time to buy.

Six months ago that house was worth $100,000. Today it's worth $110,000. Six months from now it will surely be worth $120,000. All I have to do is buy it, sit tight for a little while, and I'll make money."

The perception of increasing prices leads us to believe that the current time is a good time to buy, that we will be carried along on the crest of a wave of appreciating values.

On the other hand, when prices are declining, we tend to have opposite perceptions. "That house was worth $110,000 6 months ago. Today, it's only worth $100,000. Six months from now it will surely have fallen in value to $90,000. The best thing I can do it to stay away from it."

We tend to be buoyed by price increases and deflated by price drops. Along the way what we tend to forget is that values in real estate, as in most things, tend to be cyclical. Nothing goes up, or down, forever. This has certainly been the case historically and especially over the last 20 years in home sales.

Historical Perspective on the Housing Market

In the period between 1970 and 1990, just the last 20 years, we have had two complete real estate residential cycles in which prices went up and down. Here's how those cycles appeared (see also Figure 1-1):

1972–1975. A sluggish residential real estate market nationwide

1976–1980. A very strong up residential real estate market nationwide

1981–1985. A sluggish and declining real estate market nationwide

1986–1988. A booming real estate market in selected areas of the country

1989–present. A strong decline in the real estate market nationwide

During most of those 20 years the upward swings were far stronger than the downward moves. Only with the most recent turn in the market have we had a very strong decline.

Buying at the Wrong Time

Once we understand that the housing market recently (or historically) has not been always up (or down), the question becomes one of timing. Given the cyclical nature of the market, when is the best time to buy?

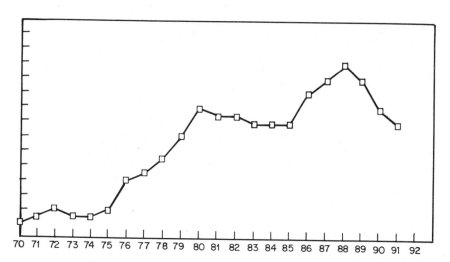

Figure 1-1. Real estate cycle. Based on price and market activity for typical U.S. residential market.

General wisdom, as noted earlier, expounds that the best time to buy is when prices are moving upward. But, this is incorrect. I have an old friend, a commodities broker, who will tell anyone who will listen that this is the *wrong* time to buy. When the market is already on the upswing, the chances of buying at the top are simply too great.

This advice is shared, I am sure, by those home buyers who purchased at the top of the recent housing market. In Los Angeles, for example, there are literally thousands of buyers who cannot as of this writing sell their home for within $50,000 to $75,000 of what they paid for it. One recent buyer whom I am acquainted with purchased her Agoura (a suburb of Los Angeles) home for $375,000 18 months ago. Today she'd be lucky to get $290,000. Try telling *her* that the right time to buy is when the market is on the upswing.

The Right Time to Buy

When, then, is the correct time to buy? In order to see when it's the right time to buy, we have to get rid of two notions. The first is an old notion, born after the Second World War, that the value of real estate always goes up. Although, as we'll see in the next chapter, because of inflation and shortages the *long-term trend* may indeed be upward, in the short run there most certainly will be both *ups* and *downs*.

The second notion to get rid of is that the cold market we've been recently experiencing is the total collapse of real estate forever. In the next chapter we'll go into specific reasons why nothing could be further from the truth. It's just as fallacious to believe that the market will go down forever as it is to believe it will go up forever.

Once we dump those two false notions, we can move forward to successful investing. Today, given recent declines, too many people believe that real estate only goes down in value. To be successful, these same people should instead be saying, "Six months ago that house was worth $110,000. Tomorrow it's going to be worth only $90,000. But the day after tomorrow it's probably going to shoot up to $150,000."

A Matter of Perception

I hope you see that in reality it's mainly a matter of perception. When prices are going up, it seems to most of us as if they must go up forever. Hence, everyone struggles to buy. On the other hand, when prices go down, one can't help but be lulled into thinking that prices will continue on down indefinitely. Therefore we shun the real estate market.

The whole point, of course, is that our perceptions are in error. There's nothing wrong with investing in the market today. It's only our perception of the market that keeps us out.

Consider. With prices going down, is now a good time or a bad time to buy real estate? I think those who see it as a bad time are wrong. To illustrate why, here's another question for you to answer. During this entire *century*, when do you think was the best *single* year to invest in real estate? It's not a trick question, although the answer is tricky.

When I ask this question of people at seminars, they typically will answer, "1979, when the market was super hot." Or, "1987, when the market in some areas increased in value by nearly 50 percent." Or, if they happen to have been around a bit longer, "1957, after the Second World War when houses jumped up in value."

These are answers of thoughtful people who want to invest. But, as noted earlier, these answers pick the best of times, the best markets in real estate. Those are not the best times to invest; they are the worst. In each case, in fact, those are the very years just before the market turned down. The best year to buy in this century wasn't even close to any of those mentioned. To my way of thinking, the best year of the century to invest in real estate was 1934.

1934? The middle of the Great Depression? Yes, and here's why. For most of those who lived through it, 1934 was not a wonderful year to remember. There were bread lines and free soup kitchens on the streets of every major city. An apple or a cup of coffee cost a nickel, but only few could afford either. And although no accurate records were kept, unemployment has been estimated to have been between 25 and 35 percent.

1934 was the depth of the depression. The stock market had collapsed in 1929. Banks began going under in 1930. By 1933 Franklin Delano Roosevelt declared a bank holiday, confiscated all private gold, and started government worker programs such as the CCC and the WPA.

Then came 1934. The banks that were left were once again on solid footing, which meant money was available for lending. However, the economy had come to a virtual halt. For real estate that meant almost no sales. Hundreds of thousands of properties were in foreclosure with no buyers. That kept the prices of all residential properties down.

Buying Low

In 1934 you could buy a home for $1000 to $3000. (Not the monthly payment, the full price.) Further, the owner would accept a paper note as the down payment and the bank would carry the rest on a roll-over basis from year to year.

You could rent out that property and as long as you kept a short leash on your tenants and collected the rent regularly, your rental income would cover most of your costs. Further, you could buy as many such rental properties as you wanted and literally pyramid your investments. After all, you were in the minority. There were very few people buying residential real estate in 1934.

Remember, it was the time of the Great Depression and the perception was that the prices of everything, and especially real estate, would never go up; they would always continue to go down.

If you bought in 1934, you were one of a group of farsighted exceptions. Your numbers include famous families like the Wrigleys, the Kennedys, and the Rockefellers. They also include individuals who really didn't have much more money than anyone else (such as my father), who also scrimped and saved and bought . . . and bought . . . and bought.

While no accurate figures of the times were kept, in perusing real estate records of the 1930s, my own observation is that there was a great consolidation of property in 1934, particularly of residential real estate. There were the same number of properties as the year before, only a lot fewer owners.

What occurred was that a few insightful investors gobbled up houses by the handful for pennies on the dollar from sellers who sold to get out before prices, as they perceived them, would go down further.

The result, of course, is history. There was an economic expansion in

1937. Then there was the Second World War and the exploding economy it produced. Finally there was the post-war economy which many consider to have ended at the beginning of the 1990s when prices of commodities, and particularly of homes, began to fall. Here's the historical picture in a nutshell: A house bought for $2000 in 1934 might be sold for:

$5000 in 1929

$4000 in 1937

$9000 in 1946

$13,000 in 1953

$25,000 in 1967

$65,000 in 1979

$100,000 in 1987 (in some parts of the country)

$75,000 in 1990

In terms of making the greatest amount of profit, by percentages, 1934 was the year. You doubled your money in just 3 years. If you hung on, of course, your profits became almost embarrassingly large.

Another Once in a Lifetime Opportunity

Well folks, we're back in 1934 again, figuratively speaking. No, the price of a home isn't $2000, but the value of the dollar isn't what it used to be either. (In the next chapters we'll examine the real value of homes when adjusted for inflation.)

With the market cold like it is today, once again we have the opportunity to buy at bargain basement prices. With sellers believing that the market can only go lower, we can make deals and get offers accepted that we only dreamed about a few years ago.

We're not looking to make 8 or 9 percent profit (currently considered a good return on investment). People who bought in 1934 weren't thinking of 10 percent profits. Buying real estate then wasn't worth the risk for 10 percent. They were thinking of doubling or tripling their money. And, of course, they succeeded. Buying in 1934 meant huge percentage increases in value down the road. For those wise enough and courageous enough to buy back then, home investment was a once in a lifetime opportunity.

That opportunity has come full circle once again. We are back to great opportunities in real estate. For those who remember the words of Parmenides—Buy low, sell high—this is again the best of times.

Prices are once again low. Opportunities to get properties at substantial reductions once again abound. We haven't seen as good a real estate market (in terms of low prices) for a very long time. (Consider, back in 1934 the dollar was worth between 25 and 30 times what it's worth today in buying power. At a *medium-priced* restaurant, a cup of coffee back then was a nickel; today it's a dollar. And a $3000 house back then is roughly a $75,000 to $90,000 house today.)

Having a Positive Outlook

It's all a matter of perception. The pessimist says the cup is half empty; the optimist sees it as half full. The doomsayer says that real estate will just go down and down. The opportunist sees today's down prices as a buying opportunity on the downward part of the cycle that can only lead up.

Where do you place yourself? Do you have the courage to see opportunity in the face of adversity? Do you want dearly enough to make your fortune to reconsider your perceptions?

In the next chapters we'll look at the reasons why the real estate market will turn around, when that's likely to happen, and what that could mean to you if you buy today.

2
Will the Market Turn Around?

There is a story about an older gentleman on the Titanic who was an irrepressible optimist. He felt that no matter how bad things got, in the end everything would work out okay. When as a passenger he learned that the Titanic, deemed the safest boat of its age, had hit a hidden iceberg on its maiden voyage, he was sure that it was simply an inconvenience. The gaping hole in the hull might slow the great ship down a bit, but it would hardly do more than that.

When the ship came to a halt and he was forced to abandon his cabin because of flooding waters, he was sure it was just a matter of getting the pumps to work and bailing out the hold. When on deck in the freezing cold with no more life boats left and the ship listing badly to one side, he felt it would just be a short time until other boats came to rescue him. And finally, as he stood on the stern watching the freezing waters engulf the boat, he believed that no matter how many others perished, he would be the one to swim to a waiting lifeboat and survive.

Of course, he drowned.

A Dim View

The moral of the tale is that optimism alone can't save a hopeless situation. Today many people are comparing the real estate market to the Titanic. They are saying that those who talk about a real estate turnaround are blind optimists, like our passenger. They point to statistics of falling prices and increasing inventories and proclaim that the situation is hopeless. Get off now because it's only going to sink.

I might be inclined to give such words more heed if I hadn't personally heard them before. They were voiced during the real estate turndowns of 1957, 1968, 1972, and 1981. After you've been through a few real estate recessions, you begin to look at them more calmly. You begin to realize that not every situation is like the Titanic. Sometimes a life raft does come by. Sometimes the boat doesn't sink.

Of course, there is always the chance that the residential real estate market may never turn around. It could simply keep dropping in a freefall. A house worth $100,000 last year could drop by $10,000 each year until, 10 years from now, it's worth nothing.

You do, however, have to be quite a pessimist to believe that. I don't know of anyone who actually does. Rather, the worst pessimists I talk with see real estate as simply declining until we reach the price levels of say, 1981 (roughly two-thirds to half of what they were in the late 1980s) and then stagnating at those levels indefinitely. They see the resurrection of the $75,000 average-priced house. Maybe even the $50,000 average-priced house.

Their attitude is that it's all over for housing as an investment. "You'd have to be crazy to buy a house today," they say. "Just rent and you'll do fine." (Interestingly many of those who are most vocal about these suggestions also happen to be deeply involved in alternative investments such as stocks and bonds.) Well dear reader, those sallow pessimists are wrong. In this chapter I aim to explain why.

A Lesson in Monetary Values

A few years ago there was a popular movie called *Back to the Future*. In Part 3 of that movie the hero, Michael J. Fox, goes back to 1885 and there with the help of co-star Christopher Lloyd gets a time machine to work, thus bringing him back to the future. It was a good movie. But as I was watching it I kept asking myself, "How did the heroes buy anything back then?"

It's one thing to take a time machine to the past. It's quite another to buy a hat or a pair of shoes or parts to fix a time machine in 1885. How did they buy anything?

This is not to say that things were expensive out west back then. A bath and a shave were probably 7 cents. A night at a hotel 20 cents. A meal might cost a dime and so forth. Things cost very little. But what did our heroes pay for them with? I don't think merchants back then accepted Visa, American Express, or Mastercard.

Today's paper money wouldn't have done very well back in 1885 either. It wouldn't be recognized or accepted, since there was virtually no paper money of any kind in the old west in those days.

Did they take back pocket change? Our "silver" coins are all virtually worthless, shiny base metal. Can you imagine a western saloon-keeper in 1885 accepting a clad Washington quarter (made of copper and nickel) in payment for a "slug of whiskey?" He'd bite the coin, determine it wasn't silver or gold, and throw the person who offered it out the door.

So, how did our heroes buy anything?

Making Purchases in 1885

The answer is real money. For example, Michael J. Fox could have used pennies—not pennies from today, but pennies from 1885.

In 1885 the accepted penny across the country was the Indian head. (It was the precursor to our current Lincoln cent.) If our heroes had the foresight to get a roll of Indian head pennies before they went ahead to the past, they probably could have done very well. One roll of pennies would undoubtedly have bought them everything needed for several days. If they happened to pick up a "double eagle" ($20 gold piece) of the period, they'd have enough money to live royally for a month or more.

Think of it, a penny actually buying something substantial instead of just weighing down your pocket with unwanted change or $20 lasting over a month. Our heroes could have lived like royalty for next to nothing.

Well, not quite. The truth of the matter is that they just couldn't go to a bank today and simply ask for, "Indian head cents, please." Or say, "I'll have a $20 gold piece." Even though those items are still authorized currency of the United States, they are available only from collectors and rare coin dealers who keep track of true value. A single Indian head cent in even modestly good condition might cost ten of today's dollars. A common date $20 gold piece could be worth close to 800 current dollars.

When comparing prices of yesterday with the present, this is the part of the story that is often overlooked. Not only did things cost far less in the past, but the very money that was used to purchase them in the past costs far more today.

In short, many things from the past that survive to the present actually retain their original buying power. Rare coins are one good example. Real estate is another.

A Piece of History

When you buy a *resale* house, condo, or co-op, you're buying a piece of the past. You're buying an item that was built 1, 3, 7, or even 47 years ago.

When you compare today's price of that older home with the price it cost brand new, you will find almost invariably that it costs more today in actual dollars than it did back then. Just like a bath or a meal or a room from 1885, the house built 10 years ago costs far more to purchase today then it did years earlier.

However, like the Indian head pennies or the double eagle $20 gold piece, that house retains its value through time. In terms of "buying power" the dollars you receive for that house today, even in a depressed market, will buy as much if not more than they did in the past when the house was first built.

Money's Loss of Value

Let's look at it from a different angle. Instead of considering that which retains buying power, such as a house, let's consider for a few moments that which loses buying power, money.

No reasonable person will argue that the value of the dollar has not declined. There are many reasons for this decline and they include the increasing size of our money supply, the borrowing that our nation does in the form of our national and foreign trade debts, and the real or controlled scarcity of certain commodities such as oil. However, no matter what the reason, the simple fact is that consistently, since the founding of our country, our money has become worth less and less in terms of what it will buy. To say it another way, it takes more and more money to buy the same item. (Of course, it hasn't been a steady decline. There have been periods of relative stability interspersed with periods of strong decline.)

The government even attempts to measure the overall decline of our currency. Each month the federal government releases the consumer price index (CPI) and the wholesale price index (WPI), which purport to measure the loss in buying power of the dollar when compared with the previous month and 12-month periods.

Tip

Don't trust what the government says in the CPI and WPI. Inflation is usually much higher. A few years ago when housing prices started moving upward very dramatically, they skewed the inflation indexes. Higher housing prices pushed the CPI rate into double digits.

In response to this the government removed the price of buying a house from the CPI and instead substituted the cost of renting, a much lower and steadier figure. Thus the CPI could show a much lower level of inflation (although a false one if you happened to be buying a house).

Recently, with housing prices declining and rental rates steadily increasing, there has been talk of changing back to the old method.

Makes you wonder, doesn't it?

The Unseen Effects of Inflation

All of the above says that something which hasn't changed in a very long time (certainly since 1885 and a lot before then) isn't likely to change in the future. Inflation has been a steady companion since the birth of our country and it's probably going to be with us for an equally long time in the future. Except for relatively short periods (such as during the great depression), it's a constant that we need to accept and deal with.

The problem is that it has become unfashionable to speak of inflation. Back in 1980 when the government's CPI showed inflation to be running at an annual rate of 12 percent, it was on everyone's lips. Recently, however, with it running around 5 percent, few people worry about it. Mention inflation and many people will yawn. They've already heard that story. But although 5 percent inflation is a lot less than 12 percent, it is still an enormous rate and can have an immense impact on pricing, particularly in real estate.

Inflation "Half Lives"

To see how inflation works in housing prices, use the following table that gives you the *half life* of different inflation rates. The *half life* is roughly equivalent to how long it takes for your money's buying power to be cut in half.

Inflation rate	4%	5%	7%	10%	12%
Approx. years to half your money	17	13	9	6	5

Since the end of World War II the rate of inflation in the United States has averaged around 5 percent. That means that every 13 years or so our money loses half its value. A 1946 dollar, in other words, is worth less than 13 cents today in buying power.

Now, what does this say for real estate? The long-term trend in inflation in this country means that when a house costs a quarter million dollars today, it isn't as much money as most of us suppose—$200,000 in terms of 1946 buying power is only about $25,000.

The Hilly Rose Show

If you think I'm crazy to say that $200,000 is not a lot of money, let me answer such astonishment with a short, true story. Back in 1976 I was a guest on talk radio shows on the subject of real estate. One of the shows I did was the Hilly Rose show, then coming out of Los Angeles. I can still remember Hilly asking me in consternation, "How can the price of a house go higher?" At the time the average price for a house in the city around $80,000, a seemingly incredible figure. It was obvious to him, as it was to most people, that prices simply couldn't go up.

I answered him in a single word, inflation. I don't think he believed me. Today the price for that house in the same area is at a minimum of $225,000. The same thing is happening again today. I'm often asked, "How can housing prices go higher? Who can afford to pay $200,000 for a home?"

I try to remind people of the fact that 45 years ago that $200,000 house was just a $25,000 house—simply on the basis of inflation alone. You see, it's a matter of perspective. Price means nothing. It's the buying power of that price.

Buying Power

Consider again the film *Back to the Future*. When Michael J. Fox was in 1885, what could he have brought back to the present that would have made him rich beyond his wildest dreams? Obviously he could have bought back some Indian head pennies and sold them for ten current dollars apiece. Or he could have brought back $20 gold pieces and sold them for 800 current dollars.

But what he could have brought back that would have made him even more fabulously wealthy is a deed. He could have brought back a deed to property in downtown Denver or Los Angeles or San Francisco. He could have brought back a deed to virtually any piece of property anywhere, bought then for perhaps $100 or less, selling today for hundreds of thousands if not millions of dollars. Can you imagine what any piece of property bought in 1885 would be worth today, anywhere at all in the country?

It's really from the perspective of the past that the true value of real estate, in this case home investment, becomes clear. If property bought in 1885 would be worth a fortune today, can it be any less true for property bought today when considered 100 years from now? 50 years? 10?

As long as we continue to have inflation and our money continues to be worth less and less, real estate will be worth more and more. It doesn't matter if real estate is in a recession in the short run. The downward fall in prices is *always* only temporary, as long as inflation continues its relentless drive into the future. Two hundred years of inflation can't be wrong. Over the long haul, real estate has a very bright future.

Fewer Can Afford to Buy Today's Home

Inflation, however, is a double-edged sword. While housing prices in general have kept up with if not exceeded inflation, salaries have not. Salary increases were in the 2 to 3 percent range while inflation was running at 4 or 5 percent. This means, in terms of buying power, that people are earning much less today than they were only 10 years ago. That's the reason that in 1980 roughly 54 percent of the population could afford the median-priced home in the United States, while by 1990 that figure was down to around 38 percent.

Thus, when people say that the problem with housing is that people can't afford to buy homes, what they are really saying is that salaries have not kept up with inflation while housing has. In short, most of the people in this country have become poorer.

A Slowdown Is What's Needed

The current slowdown and reversal in housing prices is just what's needed to allow salaries to play catch-up. Remember, it's not that salaries are going down across the United States or even remaining the same. They are going up, just at a slower pace than inflation.

Let housing remain static in price for a few years and you'll quickly see that more than half the people can once again afford a house, even if that house costs $200,000 or more.

Tip

Don't be intimidated by price. It's much like clothing. Most people aren't aware that today's *formal* clothing is really the day-to-day clothing of the last generation. Similarly most of the prices that we *are used to* are the prices the last generation paid for things.

Keep up to date. Higher prices today are, in most cases, simply a reflection of inflation, of the declining buying power of our currency. Don't fall into the trap of believing that prices could never go higher. They always do.

Housing Shortages

There's yet another reason for a rebound in housing. Residential real estate in this country has experienced long-term shortages. This fact, however, is lost on the average person who owns a home. (A HUD study in 1970 estimated that we needed to build one million *more* units than were then currently under construction until the end of the century just to keep up with need. We have fallen far below that number.)

Most of us look around and see homes everywhere. How can there be a housing shortage when there are so many houses and apartments and condos? To answer that question, just remember that houses don't last forever. The actual lifespan of a single-family dwelling is estimated by builder organizations to be between 50 and 80 years. That means that residential units built before about 1910 to 1940 (as of this writing) are reaching the end of their useful lives.

Of course, such buildings can be refurbished and modernized. You can see this happening in the fashionable areas of nearly every city from New York to San Francisco. But for every older building that is preserved, there are ten that are either bulldozed to the ground or are virtually uninhabitable. To see these you have only to travel through the vast ghettos and blighted areas of virtually every American city.

Tip

Much of the blighted housing in ghetto areas is really older, abused, and used up homes. It's often not so much that those living in such areas don't take care of their homes. It's that their homes have reached an age where it's no longer economically feasible to take care of them.

In addition, many were designed expressly as ghetto housing. Many of the tenements in Harlem, for example, are not fine older houses that have been run down by their occupants. Many were originally built to house immigrants who had little money. It was assumed in the teens and early twenties of this century that there would be five to ten people in a room and only one bath per floor. That's how landlords would make more money.

Even in California, where most housing is relatively new, entire tracts were built as future ghettos. You can see this in parts of the Santa Clara Valley, for example. The very cheapest types of construction were permitted and the houses, condos, and apartments rapidly deteriorated regardless of what their owners attempted to do in the way of upkeep.

When you subtract all the decaying residential housing (single-family and apartments) that's ending its useful life from the new that's being built, you quickly find that in most areas of the country, we're barely keeping up.

Now, add to this the enormous influx of immigrants who have come to the United States over the past several decades (primarily from Asia and South and Central America) and it doesn't take a guru to see that adequate housing isn't keeping up at all—it's falling further and further behind.

In fact another of the reasons that housing prices have gone up over the past four decades is a shortage of good, modern homes. Yes, there are plenty of houses that are falling down in blighted areas. But, if you want a relatively new home in a nice area, there's a definite shortage. The pressure to get into one of those pleasant suburban homes has helped fuel the residential real estate boom over the past 40 or so years. (New England is possibly the single exception where there has actually been a net loss of people from the area, yet more than 10 years of heavy home building.)

Shortages in a Downturn

What's important to remember is that just because housing prices have recently turned down doesn't mean that housing shortages have stopped. There are still more people than homes, more buyers than houses.

Where are they then, you may reasonably ask. Why have the buyers simply stopped buying? We have already seen part of the answer—wages which haven't kept up with inflation mean less purchasing power and fewer buyers able to qualify for mortgages on high-priced homes. There are other answers as well.

Many people are in transition (either out of work long-term or just between jobs). Many more are simply afraid to make the move to a new home at the present time because of uncertainties with the economy and their own financial health.

Finally, there is once again the matter of perception. Beginning in

1990, I believe that most people in this country really felt that we were in a recession regardless of the fact that the government's statistics showed otherwise. All they had to do was look around. Since 1989, the auto industry, the most important single employer in the country, has been in a recession. Since 1990, defense has been in a decline as high-priced spending items were cut from the budget. Since at least 1988, housing, perhaps the biggest money volume industry, has been in a severe decline. Agriculture has been in difficult straights since the early 1980s. The savings and loan and banking industries are in such a bad way that they have had to be bailed out by the government. Even consumer electronics have shown declines since 1988.

Therefore, is it any wonder that the average citizen, seeing all the declining industries around, has decided to pull back and hang tight? What difference is it to this person that through the first half of 1990 the government's gross national product (GNP) statistics continued to show increases, albeit moderate ones? (The suspicion that these figures, like the CPI, are doctored to favor the "government view" has been growing.)

The bottom line here is that it's not that there are fewer people who want to buy homes. It's that those who want to buy either can't afford to buy or are standing on the sidelines, waiting.

The important thing is not to lose sight of the fact that *we have not eliminated the housing shortage in this country.* If you want further proof, just check out the homeless camping on street corners in every city.

The truth is that we still have a large body of the population who have a strong wish to buy homes in the nicer suburbs, the intense desire to leave the crime-ridden inner cities behind. We still have people who make very good wages and whose salaries are getting better each year who can afford to buy the houses that are for sale but who are waiting.

Economic Resurgence

But when will they make their move? The answer lies in our economic health. I believe there is an economic resurgence coming. Further, I believe it will be upon us before most of us realize what's happening.

The controversial economist Ravi Batra, in a much heralded book, predicted a depression in this country beginning in 1990. The book was intensely popular, I feel, because people wanted to believe the worst. The resurgence in housing will come when people want to believe the worst is over and that the future is bright.

While there's no question that the American economy is in trouble, I believe it is far from down and out. The American economy might be likened to a boat with a damaged propeller, but it's far, far from being a Titanic.

There are many reasons why the economy will have a strong resurgence during the decade of the 1990s. While it's beyond this book to deal with them in detail, a brief summary should ring true in the minds of most readers.

Perhaps the brightest light in our economy is the reemergence of healthy industries both large and small. In the 1970s and through the 1980s, American industry suffered at the hands of the more efficient Japanese. That the Japanese could produce better products for less than America could become a truism.

The result of the intense competition with Japan, however, was a huge fallout of the less-productive American companies. Those that remain today are lean and mean. In case you hadn't noticed, American companies in the 1990s are highly competitive.

Further, higher oil prices resulting from war in the Middle East can hurt Japanese industry far more than U.S. companies. (Japan depends on 100 percent of its oil from imports. The United States imports only about 50 percent of its oil.)

In addition, there was the savings and loan scandal that dumped a great deal of residential real estate onto an already saturated market. However, as we move further into the 1990s, the savings and loan scandal will be left behind. Those lending institutions, both S&Ls and banks, which survive will be highly profitable and will be eager to make good real estate loans. The surplus of foreclosed properties will diminish and then disappear.

The backlog of properties taken back through foreclosure and held by the S&Ls ($300 billion by many estimations) is slowly being sold off as this is written. (These sales in the early 1990s offer properties at bargain basement prices. See Chapter 7 for details on how you can get one.) These properties acted to put a lid on prices in some markets and to force values down in many others. A healthy lending industry with next to no real estate owned, or REOs (foreclosed properties held for sale), emerging in the mid-1990s will mean less competition with private real estate sales and a better market resulting in escalating prices.

Finally, the inevitable raising of taxes in one form or another will help bring the federal deficit under control and thus pave the way, over the next few years, for lower interest rates. High interest rates are the single biggest drag on the real estate market. Reduced rates lower the costs of buying a home and allow more buyers (those with lower incomes) to qualify and enter the market, thus promoting an upswing.

The Coming Real Estate Turnaround

In short, there is every reason to believe that the decade of the 1990s, once the first few troubled years are past, will turn into another real estate boom. There's every reason to think that home buyers will again return in swarms to the housing market. And the housing market will again take off as it has so many times in the past.

When you put it all together—continued inflation, lower prices allowing wages to catch up, continued housing shortages, and a coming resurgence in the economy—the bottom line is that the residential real estate market, as black as it may look today, will turn around with a roar in the next few years.

However, what I personally believe should be irrelevant to you. It's what you believe that counts. The reason is simple; if you believe in a real estate turnaround, you'll be willing to spend your money, exert your efforts, and commit your time. On the other hand, if you are a Titanic thinker and feel this is all empty prattle, then quite frankly, there's no reason for you to continue reading this book. If you believe (in your heart if not in your mind) that we are on the brink of a bottomless pit in terms of real estate, immediately get a one-way ticket to some far off less-troubled land (if one exists). This book can do you no good. You won't be able to benefit from the information it contains.

Only if you understand that the real estate market historically has been cyclical and that we are currently in a down cycle with an up cycle to follow can this book show you how to make a profit.

There are no profits to be made if the market simply spirals ever lower and lower. There is money, however, big money to be made by buying low and selling high as our friend Parmenides demonstrated in the last chapter.

But to take advantage, you have to be committed to the resilience and spring-back ability of American real estate. If you don't see a turnaround coming, you won't have the courage necessary to make the investments today that will reap you a fortune tomorrow.

Picking the Bottom

Okay, let's suppose you agree, if for no other reason than for the sake of argument, that the real estate market, as bad as it is today, will turn around. There's only one really big question you have to answer—when? When will it turn around and when will prices begin soaring back up? That's the subject of the next chapter.

3
Picking
the Bottom

Many stock and commodity market investors say that trying to pick bottoms and tops of markets can be a fool's game. Your chances of being wrong are too great. They suggest its far safer to wait until the market turns before making your investment. Their reasoning is that this way you have a much higher chance of making a profit, albeit a smaller one, than if you try to pick the bottom.

The problem with this reasoning, of course, is that by the time everyone is convinced that the market has turned around, it's generally too late to get on board. This is particularly the case with real estate. The real bargains occur when people are convinced the market is headed down. As soon as the general consensus is that it has turned around, not only do prices begin to accelerate, but the terms sellers demand get far tougher and in real estate, sometimes terms can be more important than price.

Tip

Many people in real estate believe that you make your profit not when you sell but when you buy. I think it's a bit of both, but buying when the market is down doesn't hurt.

Thus, if you plan to invest in today's cold real estate market, it will behoove you to have some strong indications of when the market has bottomed out. Keep in mind that because real estate is such an illiquid commodity, it lacks volatility. The bottom may last 6 months to a year or

25

s compared to perhaps a few days in stocks and a few hours in
_____dities.

While no one can predict with complete accuracy when the real estate
market has bottomed out, there are certain indicators which will suggest
that point. Very few people, however, seem to be aware of these, so if you
know them, you'll have a real advantage.

Residential Real Estate Is a Different Market

In order to understand how the indicators of a residential market bottom work, it's necessary to first have some special knowledge of that market. It's important to know that this market is not like the markets for
gold or soybeans or automobiles or electronic parts. Nothing else in the
world operates quite like the residential real estate market. Here's why.

Let's say that you are an orange grower. You have a grove of orange
trees and it's summertime and you're picking the fruit. You need to
bring your crop to market. Only the market this year happens to be terrible. Orange juice prices are way down. If you sell, you not only won't
make a profit, you'll actually lose money. What do you do?

Well, your choices are to sell or not to sell. If you don't sell, you can
dump the crop in the ocean or bury it underground or grind it up into
orange juice and then freeze it hoping for a better market next year. The
trouble with all of these alternatives is that they mean you will lose the
value of your crop and probably go broke.

So, in spite of the bad market, you sell, even if it means selling at a loss.
You recoup at least some of your money, hoping to do better next year.
In the process, however, you depress the market even further.

Now let's say that instead of orange juice, you're an automobile dealer
and Detroit has just sent you fifty cars, only there just aren't any buyers.
You are paying interest on bank loans on every one of those cars. You
can't send them back to Detroit because the manufacturer doesn't want
them—it's preparing to crank out next year's models.

So what do you do? Your choices are to go out of business or sell the
cars, even if you have to make deals at or below your actual costs. As with
the orange juice, your dumping the cars on the market depresses auto
prices even further.

I hope, dear reader, that my feeble attempts to illustrate market conditions make the point. What I am trying to get at is that if you are selling
orange juice or cars or almost anything else, you have a "wasting product." That means that you have to sell or your product's value wastes
away. In the case of oranges, they spoil. In the case of cars, there's the
interest charges plus the fact that next year's models will make the cur-

rent models obsolete. In other words, you are between a rock and a hard place. You really have no choice but to sell.

That's the way it is with most commodities—but not with residential real estate. Historically speaking, the market for homes (and condos and co-ops) is quite different, almost unique.

What Makes Residential Real Estate Different?

The thing that makes residential real estate (houses, condos, and co-ops) so different from other commodities, in terms of the necessity to sell, is that they are also homes. The vast majority are owner occupied (nearly 60 million at last count).

This makes all the difference in the world. When the market is down, in most cases (certainly not all, but most), these owners have a choice that the orange grower and the car dealer did not have. These home owners can *choose* not to sell at all and to withdraw the house from the market. In fact, in a cold market the *vast majority* of sellers do eventually choose to withdraw rather than sell at a perceived loss. (I say "perceived" because usually a seller's opinion of profit or loss depends on the *highest* price a similar house ever sold for.)

A Real Life Example

I have some friends in Southern California and they illustrate this point. Dave and Debra wanted to sell their house in an affluent area. Houses like theirs had sold for as high as $350,000 only a year earlier. But the market had fallen apart. Being more realistic than many others, they put theirs up for sale at $319,000. They expected a quick sale at the low price.

But the number of houses available (called "in inventory" in the trade) was high and there were few buyers. When, after 3 months their house not only hadn't sold, but they had not had a single offer, their agent suggested they lower their price. They were told the market for their homes was now around $285,000. They would have to drop their price $34,000 in order to sell.

Did they drop? No, they simply took their house off the market. They had wanted to sell in order to buy a home closer to town. Now they were willing to forego that desire rather than lose money.

Dave and Debra are not alone. As noted, *most* home sellers act the same way. Unless they must sell because of a compelling reason (such as a job-forced move or financial problems), most people simply withdraw their offer to sell their house. (In Chapter 6 we'll examine how to find those sellers who are compelled to sell and who will give you a bargain basement price.)

Dave and Debra's reasoning is simple. They have to live somewhere. It's not costing them any more to live where they are than to move. So, they'll simply wait out the downturn in the market.

Unlike oranges and automobiles, in a cold market, houses (and condos and co-ops) are often withdrawn from sale if the seller cannot obtain a minimum desired price. That's what makes residential real estate so different from other markets. Instead of supply and demand driving prices down until they absolutely bottom out, beyond a certain point the supply simply shrinks and this acts to stabilize the price.

Thus to recap, in a down residential real estate market what typically happens is that prices initially fall. After a period of time, however, sellers reach a point where they simply refuse to sell at a lower price and take their homes off the market. At that point prices begin to stabilize.

Price Stability

Once prices stabilize because sellers have withdrawn homes for sale, the most likely possibility is that this period of stability will last until the market turns around. This period might be as short as 6 months to a year, as was the case in 1958 and 1973. Or it might be much longer as was the case in 1981 to 1986 when in many areas of the country it lasted 5 years.

During this period of stability housing prices may drift slightly lower, but there should be no dramatic drops. Too many owners will be pulling their homes off the market to have the price fall significantly.

Tip

In a stabilized but low market, the real bargains to be had may not only be in price but also in terms. You may be able to pick up homes with vastly reduced interest rates on their mortgages (carried back by the sellers). You may find that sellers will accept much lower down payments. Or you may find that in terms of a distressed property (a "fixer-upper") you can get a real bargain in terms of all three: price, down payment, and terms.

For most of the remainder of this chapter we'll be talking about a stabilized cold market. However, at the end of the chapter, we'll discuss a different kind of market, one that has "blown out."

Picking the Bottom

So, how do you know when the market has stabilized, has hit bottom? There is a way to tell that is usually quite accurate but, as I said earlier, it is relatively unknown to most people. It's to compare inventories with sales.

Inventories are the number of houses that are for sale at any given time. You can find the current inventory in your area by checking with real estate brokers or with your local real estate board. In virtually all metropolitan communities Realtors® are computerized and have instant access to this information. They can give you comparisons of inventory between this month and last, and this year and last, as well as many other useful figures. They can also give you sales figures and comparisons of these between last month, and last year and so forth.

Compare inventories and sales. In a typical slump a curve emerges. As noted earlier, inventories will begin to grow as buyers diminish. When the news that prices aren't going up anymore gets out (via the local newspapers who always run such stories), those sellers who were considering moving immediately put their houses on the market to sell before the slump. (Of course, they are too late.) Even though inventories are growing, sales begin to decline.

Declining sales cause inventories to swell and actually works to produce the slump. However, at this point prices typically remain high. Sellers, remembering recent sales at high prices, continue to try to get those values. This is really the beginning of the downward pull.

As time progresses, usually 6 months to a year with relatively few sales and ever-increasing inventories, prices begin to tumble. Those sellers who are desperate slash their prices to get out. Again the newspapers herald this event and as a result, buyers only make "low-ball" offers, thus cutting prices even further.

The market now enters a free-fall with buyers demanding and getting ever lower prices. It is usually at this point that the inventory is at or near its maximum point. However, by now sellers who haven't been able to sell at the price they want and who aren't compelled to move begin taking their homes off the market. As we noted earlier, residential real estate is unique. Most sellers would rather hold than sell at a price they perceive to be low.

Thus, even though prices are falling, inventory begins to shrink. When the inventory of unsold homes shrinks to the point at which there are sufficient buyers to keep it stable, you're at the bottom of the market (see Figure 3-1). Prices stabilize and now's the time to go "bottom fishing."

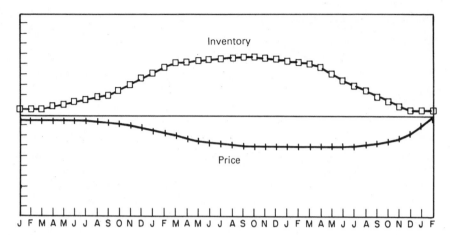

Figure 3-1. Bell curve showing market fall—inventory versus price. Inventory is the inverse of price.

How to Track the Market

As I noted, keep up on inventories and the number of sales; both figures are available from realtors. When you see inventories growing, don't buy. That's on the way down, not the bottom.

But when you see inventories shrinking and, at the same time, see the number of sales remaining low, you are close to stabilization. Prices will probably bottom out there. You're at the typical bottom of a residential real estate slump.

How long with the bottom last? That depends on other factors discussed in the last chapter. Inflation, interest rates (low rates help real estate by allowing more buyers to qualify), the health of the economy, and the pressure of buyers in a housing market are all factors.

My personal opinion is that given current conditions we should see a significant turnaround by the end of 1992 or the beginning of 1993 at the latest. If my prediction is accurate, you don't have a very long time to find those bargains and buy them.

A Market Blow-Out

There is another type of residential real estate slump and that occurs when instead of stabilizing, the market goes into a free-fall. It doesn't happen very often, but it did occur in Texas in 1987 and in Arizona in

1988 and 1989. The inventory did not diminish and prices just kept on falling until, in many cases, they were half or less of what they had been before.

I am sure many readers are wondering how this can occur when I've just said that as prices fall, sellers take their homes off the market thus reducing inventory and stabilizing prices. How can a blow-out occur given this fact?

The answer is that sometimes sellers have to sell no matter what. In the case of Texas, when the oil money dried up from the reduced oil prices of the mid-1980s, hundreds of thousands of people were thrown out of work. The mass joblessness meant that a large proportion of them simply had to sell.

Too many houses came onto the market too fast and, because the sellers were compelled to get out, were not withdrawn. Those sellers who could not sell very frequently lost their homes through foreclosure. Taken back, mostly by savings and loans, these houses remained on the market as the lenders tried to get rid of them.

Thus in the Texas market a big drop in the economy forced a blow-out in housing. Even a turnaround in oil prices in 1990 did not instantly cure the situation.

In Arizona it was simply overbuilding and speculating. Phoenix is the prime example. Phoenix has always had one thing in ample supply, land. Developers would no sooner complete one project then they would start building homes on another. Since rosy projections showed nearly half a million people a year moving into the city, no one complained—until those newcomers didn't arrive.

When the projected population didn't coincide with the real population, there was suddenly an enormous surplus of unsold housing. Builders began dumping their homes. Unable to sell in a slumping market, whole tracts were foreclosed upon and taken back by lenders who then put them onto the market. Speculators who had bought houses hoping to take advantage of the coming boom were also compelled to sell.

As a result, just as in Texas, the inventory kept growing in spite of lowering prices and a blow-out occurred. The market literally collapsed. It wasn't until most of the states' S&Ls were declared insolvent and taken over by the government and, as a result, loan money for the construction of new homes was cut off that the surplus began to slowly diminish and prices began to stabilize.

A blow-out is rare, but it can occur. You can watch for it. Keep your eye on those inventories. If they continue to increase while sales continue to decline, watch out—it's going to be a long while before stabilization occurs.

Tip

_____

Don't invest in real estate when inventories of unsold homes are increasing. Wait until those inventories begin to go down and prices stabilize. But be careful. If you wait too long and word gets out that a turnaround has occurred, you could miss out on the bottom.

Bottom Hunting

Because the bottom lasts so long in the residential real estate market, relative to other investments, it's good hunting even for the casual investor. It doesn't take a lot of time to track inventories and prices. But be sure you do it yourself. Don't trust the newspapers or brokers to do it for you. Their errors or failures to keep good track could cost you your opportunity.

4
The Buy, Rent, & Hold Strategy

During the Second World War, the Japanese had control of most of the strategic islands in the Pacific almost all the way to Hawaii. At the time the Japanese military command, and most of the American military command as well, figured it would take half a decade for the United States to take those islands. It was envisioned that the U.S. Marines and the U.S. Navy would have to fight for each island, winning the first in order to launch an invasion of the second and so forth. Along the way, the Japanese hoped, the United States would lose its enthusiasm for war and settle for a negotiated peace.

Fortunately for the United States, the general in charge of operations was Douglas MacArthur. Although much maligned for his public relations failures at home, MacArthur was certainly the most creative military strategist in the Pacific during the war. He developed a plan whereby instead of taking one island after another, he hopscotched over the islands taking every other one or every third or fourth one, isolating those in between.

His strategy, according to many historians, shortened the war in the Pacific by as much as 3 years and saved as many as a million lives on the American side alone. When MacArthur was asked what the key element of his plan was, he replied in a single word, guts.

MacArthur was willing to risk sending men essentially behind the enemy lines to take a position and then hold it until his main forces could catch up. This strategy of invading, digging in, and holding resulted not only in shortening the war, but in realizing ultimate victory. It's also a strategy that works well for real estate in a cold market.

Buy, Rent, & Hold

The idea is simple, although as we'll see in this book, the application isn't always as easy. In order to make money, to be successful in a cold real estate market, you need to do three things:

1. Buy properties, preferably single-family residences at reduced, bargain basement prices
2. Aggressively rent out those properties for enough money to pay for most of your costs
3. Hold onto those properties until the market catches up with you and you can sell, ideally, for strong profits

It does, of course, take some cash, but not as much as you might think since many lenders in a cold market are very eager to help you get into properties by making favorable mortgages. It takes some effort to rent aggressively, which means being sure the tenant pays on time or finding a new tenant. And holding takes a certain amount of guts when you can't clearly see the light at the end of the tunnel (when you can't see the market immediately turning around).

But the payoff can be enormous. When the market does turn around, you won't be making 10 or 15 percent profit on your properties. You should be making 50 percent or more.

Note: You can follow this strategy when buying a dozen or a hundred properties—or just one. If you want to get started in real estate but don't want to make a huge commitment of time, money, and energy, just concentrate on buying, renting, and holding one house. The amount you make when the turnaround comes should well reward your efforts.

While the strategy seems simple enough, the pitfalls along the way can be menacing. Let's take a closer look at what's involved.

Buy Low

The first element is to buy low. If you can buy low, you can later turn around and sell high. This is, obviously, the key to making profits. (As noted in an earlier chapter, many investors feel that the real profit is made by buying at the right price.)

In a cold market, buying low isn't terribly difficult, if you can correctly judge the bottom (see the last chapter). Most sellers are desperate and the trick is to find a seller who's realistic about the market. (See Chapter 6 for tips on finding just such a seller.)

But buying low also means that you must be able to act quickly. The best way to do this is to have a line of credit established beforehand. This can be either unsecured credit from a bank (difficult to get) or secured credit based on the house you are getting (much easier to get). We'll have much more to say about this in Chapter 11.

Finally, buying low means looking for homes in the better areas. Better areas will still command a higher price than less desirable ones in a cold market, but they're usually worth it in terms of rentability and later salability.

Trap

Don't be penny wise and pound foolish. In a cold market, shoddy areas of town, particularly those that are in or near ghetto areas, will really come down in price. Their costs will be a fraction of what a house in a better area will cost. The temptation will be to buy a "blue collar" house for $50,000 rather than try to get one in an upgraded area for $80,000.

As a general rule, go for the more expensive house in the better area even if you have to strain to get it. The reason is simple. When the market turns, the house in the better neighborhood will go up faster and will command a higher price, sooner.

Risks Involved in Buying Low. There are risks involved in attempting to buy low. These include the following:

1. You might not pick the bottom of the market. Prices might fall *after* you buy.
2. You might buy low but still pay so much for the property that it cannot support itself on the rental income.
3. You might overextend yourself and find that you have to lower your lifestyle in order to come up with the money to make the purchase.

Rent Aggressively

There are no "nice guys" when it comes to being a landlord. Renting aggressively means that you rent fairly, you offer a property that's clean and in good condition, and you do any maintenance work that it needs. But it also means that you demand to be treated fairly. You insist that the rent be paid on time and if it isn't, the tenant moves out, no excuses accepted. It also means that if there's any damage or anything is left dirty, the tenant picks up the tab.

Renting aggressively can be difficult or easy depending on your temperament and it's good to know in advance just what your temperament is. If you are the sort of person who feels sorry for the plight of other people, who always stands ready to help out when someone else is in trouble, you'll probably make a terrible landlord. Over time your tenants will discover your temperament and many will surely seek to take advantage of you.

On the other hand, if you're a callous sort of person who is indifferent to the plight of others, you too may make a poor landlord. Your tenants will quickly catch on to your attitude and will go out of their way to outsmart or cheat you.

The ideal landlord is someone who does care but, most important of all, is fair. This landlord sets out his or her rules and then sticks by them. If it's possible to help a tenant by, for example, allowing an extra person to reside in the property or permitting the tenant to have a dog or even by letting the tenant store some furniture in an unused garage, this landlord will help. But this landlord also expects the tenant to do his or her share. When the rent is due, it must be paid. If it's not paid, the tenant must move out so the property can be rented to someone else who can pay. In short, although it's difficult, you can be both a human being and a landlord.

Tip

Having spent at least 30 years as a landlord, I can tell you from long experience that most people are honest and reliable. They will keep the property clean and pay their rent on time.

On the other hand, there are those few others will take every advantage they can get. It's important not to let these others get away with it. When a tenant comes in saying they just can't pay their rent, I'm simply not very sympathetic. I know that most people have some savings or have relatives or friends who can help out in a tough situation. They should call on their savings, relatives, and friends before calling on me to help them out.

I also know that many people who rent simply are not very good at budgeting their money. Some will spend more than they have. Others simply won't be able to keep track of their funds. As a result, they will occasionally be in the position of "robbing Peter to pay Paul." I want to be sure that in this case, I'm not Peter.

The Landlord's Nightmare. There will come a time, if you have enough properties or rent long enough, when you will get into the worst possible situation. You'll have a tenant who won't move and won't pay.

Be aware that this will be your worst nightmare. You won't be receiving rent and in order to get the tenant out, you will have to press an "unlawful detainer" action in court. Further, when the tenant moves, the place can be a shambles.

Renting aggressively means being sure that this nightmare doesn't happen or that it happens as rarely as possible. This means that you will get a credit report on every tenant, you will check with previous landlords for references, and you will get a big up-front security and cleaning deposit. (We'll have much more to say about this in Chapter 12.)

In short, renting aggressively means that you refuse to be a patsy. You treat your property as you would a business and your goal is to make a profit (or at least to break even).

Hold for the Turnaround

The bottom line to all of this, of course, is that down the road a few years you anticipate a turnaround. The real estate market in your area will stop being sluggish and slow and will again begin moving upward. At that time, you'll sell for a profit.

Here's an example of someone who's doing just that. I have a real estate investor friend in Phoenix who is currently flying very high. Phyllis is making money hand over fist in a market that is beginning to turn around. But, she has yet to sell one of the over seventeen properties she has acquired over the past 3 years. Phyllis works hard and makes the right moves.

Arizona, you may recall, was one of the hardest hit states in the real estate recession. Vast amounts of land kept prices low. Fat savings and loans made ridiculously generous mortgages to builders, who threw up hundreds of subdivision houses. Overbuilding and overspeculation were rampant.

Eventually, the piper had to be paid. Seven out of ten of the state's largest S&Ls became insolvent and were taken over by the government. Huge numbers of homes were left unsold, deserted, unwanted. The situation was reminiscent of Texas at the bottom of the oil recession when whole tracts of unsold homes lay vacant, open to vandalization.

It was into this market that Phyllis strode ready to make her fortune. She bought REOs (foreclosures) from S&Ls. She bought homes at auction. She bought from individuals who were moving out, sometimes for as little as a down payment of $10. She got real bargains, buying houses for half their former value.

Acquiring the property, however, turned out to be the easy part. The rental market had likewise collapsed. Thousands of home owners, finding they couldn't sell, put their homes up for rent. The Phoenix papers were running dozens of pages of tiny ads for apartments, condos, and houses.

After awhile the tenants caught on. They demanded bonuses to move in. They wanted the first and last month's rent *free*. They wanted a TV set or a microwave. They wanted no cleaning deposits.

Phyllis aggressively rented in this market. She dropped her price below the competition even though for awhile it caused her to have a negative cash flow (the properties brought in less money than they cost). She insisted on a good credit report, references, and at least the first month's rent and a cleaning deposit.

The interesting thing was that she got the good tenants. Those tenants who were interested in the long haul looked for low rent. Those who were just there to hop from property to property for free months' rent and bonus awards looked elsewhere.

By working hard, borrowing from her savings and later from relatives, she hung onto each of her properties. Then, when the market turned, she raised the rents. Eventually she refinanced some of her properties to get cash out. When the market in Phoenix does finally swing up again, Phyllis will be in a terrific position to take advantage of it. Can you imagine her profits when she sells seventeen houses which might just double or more in value?

Holding Indefinitely

Phyllis exemplifies the person who plans to hold real estate and then sell. I have another friend, a broker in Denver, however, who buys distressed property and then simply rents it out, indefinitely. Using an exemption in the tax laws (described in Chapter 13), he is able to depreciate the property and write the paper loss off against his regular income. His theory is simply that if he holds the property long enough, the tenants will pay off the mortgage and he'll have it free and clear. He can then keep most of the rental income for himself or, if he needs money, he can refinance like Phyllis.

Both kinds of holding work.

Can You Do It?

As I mentioned with my opening example of Douglas MacArthur, the whole strategy of buy, rent, and hold works *if* you have the guts to do it. The real question, therefore, is do you have the guts?

You've now been introduced to the market conditions that suggest you will be able to find properties at distressed prices (Chapter 1). You've been given the arguments that suggest a turnaround will be coming soon (Chapter 2). You've had a taste of what buying low, renting aggressively, and holding involves (this chapter). Now, I'm asking you to make a decision. Is this for you or not?

There should be no embarrassment in deciding not to pursue the dream of creating a fortune for yourself in real estate. Some people really are satisfied to remain where they are financially. You may have a good paying job that is quite secure. Without a doubt, pursuing the strategy I've outlined takes some time and effort (although it certainly isn't a full-time job—usually just a few hours a week). Perhaps you simply don't want to make the effort or take the time. Or perhaps you are doing so well that the rewards don't seem sufficiently appealing. (You have to be doing amazingly well to justify this last.) If that's the case, put this book down. You won't find anything more of value in it for you.

On the other hand, if your determination to make money exceeds your hesitation to try something different or if you've invested in real estate before and you want to broaden your horizons, please move onward. In the following pages we'll cover the techniques you need to perfect in order to buy, rent, and hold—and then sell for an embarrassingly large profit.

5
Seven Rules for Buying Right

Not long ago I was in Paris and I wanted to walk from my hotel in a nearby suburb to the Champs Élysées, the main boulevard of the city. I had a map, but the street names were all unfamiliar and when I tried taking this street or that, I invariably found that they tended to dead end, something the map did not show.

So I asked passersby for directions in my halting French. Henry Higgins (*My Fair Lady*) may have been right when he said that the French don't care what they do, as long as they pronounce it properly. My halting high-school and college French produced mostly disdain. Those who took pity and did give me directions gesticulated wildly pointing this way and that and rattling off street names that I couldn't catch.

I walked for several hours before concluding that I simply couldn't get from where I was to the Champs Élysées. Eventually I gave up walking and took a taxi (which got me there in less than 10 minutes).

What does my Paris experience have to do with real estate? Simply this. If you've read this far, you are probably enthusiastic about taking advantage of the current low prices in housing. However, translating that enthusiasm into profitable action may be more difficult. Yes, you may be saying to yourself, there are bargains to be had and I want them. But what do I do now? How do I get from where I am (wanting to get involved in real estate) to where I want to be (successfully buying property)? If you're new to investing in real estate (or even if you've invested before but find the current market different from what you're used to), you're somewhat like me in Paris—lost.

In this chapter you're going to get found. We're going to discuss seven

41

rules for buying right. Follow these rules assiduously and, while they probably won't lead you to the Champs Élysées, I guarantee they will bring you to the kind of properties that can make you some serious money. These rules are:

1. Never look far from home
2. Buy single-family housing
3. Look for strong tenant markets
4. Only buy property with a good price/rent ratio
5. Know what your expenses will be
6. Get favorable terms
7. Be sure that you get a bargain price and not an inflated value

Now, let's consider each separately.

Rule 1—Never Look Far from Home

I like to think that after 30 years in real estate, I've made all of the mistakes. I've made this one, as well, once. However, the reason I list it first is because it's the single biggest problem that people come to me to discuss. When people have problems with their property, everything has an answer, except this. For this problem the only solution is to not buy into it in the first place.

Consider, when you buy a stock or a bond, do you care where the company issuing it is located? You may be living in Atlanta, Georgia, and the company may be in Fairbanks, Alaska. Does that matter? It shouldn't. As a stock- or bondholder, you are in no way involved in the company's operation. Your only concern is that it make money and pay its debts. As a consequence, where the company is physically located is irrelevant.

Real estate, however, is different. When you invest in real estate as a small investor, you are directly involved in operations. You are the person who has to solve the day-to-day problems of leaky faucets, tenants who won't pay, or lawns that need mowing. If you're far away, even small tasks can mushroom into big problems. Consider the following true example.

Jake's Investment House

Jake was aware of the real estate bargains that are available. He decided, however, that more was better. He lived in California where the market was down. However, he was aware that in neighboring Arizona, the market was not only down, but blown out. In Los Angeles (where he lived), even in a cold market it would cost him upward of $200,000 to buy an investment home. In Phoenix, he could buy a home of roughly the same size for under $50,000.

The lower price, he reasoned, made it easier to buy and involved less out-of-pocket cash for the down payment. In addition when the market finally turned around he stood to make far greater profits in Phoenix.

His reasoning was correct on both counts. Where he erred was in forgetting that it takes about 12 hours to drive from Los Angeles to Phoenix or about a couple hundred dollars in air fare and car rentals (depending on the rate wars then in effect).

Jake went ahead and bought not one, but two houses in Phoenix. Since he couldn't be there to directly take care of them, he hired a property manager, a real estate broker who took care of properties for out-of-state owners. The broker only charged Jake $30 a house for property management with the understanding than when it came time to sell, Jake would give the broker the listings. Jake counted the low charge as an extra bonus.

Jake bought the houses, told the broker to rent them, and left counting his future profits. He thought nothing more about it until the end of the month when his first monthly mortgage payments came due. He called the broker and asked where the rent money was so that he could make the payments. The broker responded that only one house had been rented. The other was still vacant. In addition, he had spent all the rental income in painting and cleaning the two houses. There was no rental income left to send to Jake.

Jake grumbled a lot as he took the money out of his personal account and made the mortgage payments.

The next month there was no money again. This time the broker explained the second house was rented, but the tenants in the first were refusing to pay. He had hired an attorney and was attempting to evict them under an unlawful detainer action. The lawsuit would cost about $1500 and could Jake please send half the money immediately.

Jake wanted to go to Phoenix and ring the broker's neck for putting in such a bad tenant. However, he was occupied with work and couldn't take the time off, so he sent the money instead.

The third month when no money came he learned the first tenant had been evicted. However, that tenant had done $2000 damage to the house. Even when the rent from the second home was applied, Jake had to send in another $1500 to cover the costs. Jake put his work down and flew to Phoenix.

The first house was a mess and needed new painting in and out plus new carpeting. Jake pointed out that it was a small house and he and his son could paint it out in a few days. Go ahead, the broker said. Jake reminded himself that he had to be at work. He left exhorting the broker to do better.

The next month both houses were rented and Jake received a rent payment from both that covered his mortgages. He began to relax. Things were working themselves out. However, the month after that the air conditioning unit on the second house went out and the broker wanted an immediate $1400 to fix it. Jake refused saying the price was outrageous. He could get an air conditioner fixed in California for $300.

A week later the tenants moved out saying they couldn't stay in a house in Phoenix in the summer (where the temperature is frequently over 110 degrees) without air conditioning. The broker indicated he couldn't rerent it until the air conditioner was fixed. And, by the way, the broker continued, he was taking a new job in Texas and so this would be his last month. Jake would have to find someone else to handle the rentals.

Jake drove to Phoenix. He found that the only other broker who would take the properties wanted $75 per house per month. Jake grabbed at it because he had to get the matter settled and get back to work.

This sad saga actually goes on for 2 years. Jake only put $5000 down to buy both houses. But during those ensuing 2 years he forked out another $18,000 to maintain them. At the end of that time he sold his equity in one house for $2500 and his equity in the other for $50. His experience had cost him $20,000 before taxes. Yet he credited himself with being lucky to get out. At least now he could sleep at nights.

Avoiding Rental Problems

The best way to avoid the kind of rental problems that Jake had is to buy close to home. If possible, buy an investment house within a half hour's drive of your home. More than an hour and you could be in trouble.

If you're close by, you can put an ad in the paper and rent the property yourself. If something goes wrong, you can fix it yourself or hire out the work to people you know and trust. If a tenant doesn't pay, you can be right there and talk with the tenant to find out what the problem is. In short, there's no alternative to being right on the spot when you have a real estate problem.

I have a real estate attorney friend who handles hundreds of units. He gave me the only exception to the above rule. It's this—if you have 20 units or more, you may be able to handle it as an absentee landlord.

With those many units as a minimum, you can afford to hire a manager who will take good care of your properties. With less than 20 units, you can't command the undivided attention of a manager. Consequently, you need to do it yourself.

You Can Do It

It's important not to get the wrong message from Jake's story. I'm not trying to say that renting real estate is a horrible, impossible task; 95 percent of all problems can be handled in just a few minutes, if you care enough to do it right. If you're there, you can pick the right tenants. You can do minor work yourself. You can hire out major work to people who you know and can get recommendations on.

In short, being there makes the difference. I have rented property for at least 30 years and have never come across a problem I couldn't quickly and easily handle myself. On the other hand, the one time I bought property across the country and relied on a property manager, I had nothing but problems. They weren't as severe as Jake's, but they were nothing to sneeze at either.

Rule 2—Buy Single-Family Housing

It's important to understand that as of this writing all aspects of the real estate market are down in most areas. This includes not only residential but also commercial, industrial, and offices.

If you contact the Resolution Trust Corporation (RTC) (discussed in Chapter 7), you will find that the number of single-family houses that they have is not huge. Most of the value of their properties lies in the other areas, in small "strip" centers, in office buildings, and in some industrial parks. As a consequence, you may be tempted to branch off into these other areas of real estate. Don't do it.

Industrial, commercial, and office space are highly specialized areas of real estate which have cycles which may or may not correspond to those of housing. Markets are difficult to gauge and values difficult to judge. Rental incomes can be easily manipulated to appear higher than they really are. Location can be even more important than it is for housing. Unless you are a sophisticated investor or can afford to pay big bucks for good management, stay away from everything but residential real estate.

Which brings us to the type of residential real estate to consider. Obviously, I like houses. The reason is that they are easy to buy (financing is readily available as we'll discover). They are easy to rent (most people prefer them to any other type of housing). They are comparatively easy to maintain. And when it comes time to resell, you get the highest profits.

Condos

Beware of condos. The temptation to buy may prove nearly irresistible, since these are typically offered at lower prices than houses. For example, you can usually buy a condo for 50 to 80 percent of the price of a single-family home. In addition, a condo will often rent for 80 to 90 percent of the cost of a single-family home. It may seem very appealing to buy a low-cost, high rental income condo instead of a home.

Historically, however, condos perform the worst of any residential real estate. In a cold market they fall first and go lower. In an up market, they are the last to rebound and their price increases are the slowest. The fact of the matter is simply that people (potential buyers) don't see the value in condos that they do in homes. For most people, condos are a second choice. They get a condo *only* if they can't get a house.

There are many reasons for this but most come down to the fact that the drawbacks usually offset the benefits. Let's consider the benefits. These include common areas (such as the lawn in front) which are wholly taken care of by the home owners association (HOA), recreational facilities such as a spa or pool, and lower initial and ongoing costs.

Now the drawbacks: Typically you have no garage, neighbors are only a thin wall away, and there can be parties and noise outside that keep you awake. In short, condo living is much like living in an apartment. (Many condos are, in fact, converted apartment buildings.) And why would anyone want to pay a purchase price to live in an apartment?

Most people apparently feel the drawbacks of condos outweigh the advantages and, hence, they opt for a single-family home. This means that although you will have to pay more initially for a single-family home, when it comes time to resell, you'll almost always end up getting a much higher price.

Tip

If you're still considering a condo, don't overlook the "hidden costs." These include HOA dues. When you rent a house out, the tenant typically takes care of the lawn and garden. When you rent out a condo, the HOA does and bills you. These days most HOAs have discovered that realistic costs mean that they need to charge in the neighborhood of $300 a month or more for dues. That's a charge you don't have with a single-family house.

Duplexes, Triplexes, Flats, Etc.

There are a variety of small multiple-dwelling buildings that are for sale that go under a variety of names. Usually the idea here is that you combine the best of both worlds. You buy a home for yourself, then rent part of it out to someone else. The thought is that the rental income helps offset the cost. You have both a home and an investment property.

In reality you end up with the worst of both possible worlds. You don't really have a home because your tenant is right next door. Do you really want to live right next door to your tenant? (He or she will be over every second with complaints.) In addition you don't really have a good rental because you're not able to offer a single-family *detached* home that can command top dollar. Instead, you're offering a kind of cross between condo and apartment.

An Exception to the Rule

In some urban areas near the center of cities, multiple units can pay off. When single-family detached becomes outrageously expensive, they can be a good alternative. I've seen this in San Francisco, Oakland, New York, Boston and other major cities. But be careful.

Co-ops

Co-ops have somewhat the same characteristics as condos. However co-ops, which are primarily located on the East Coast, were often built in prime locations in the heart of cities, which results in a strong demand for them.

Co-ops, in my opinion, as a real estate rental investment usually don't really make a lot of sense (there are exceptions). In most co-ops there are restrictions against renting that make it difficult to get tenants. In addition the other co-op owners may object to the point where you'll find it's easier to sell than to rent. Finally, the legal structure of a co-op (you own a share of a corporation as opposed to a fee simple title) may make renting impractical.

Apartment Buildings

Apartment buildings are a mixed bag for the investor. I have seen some which have made incredible, mind boggling profits. Unfortunately, I've seen others with roughly the same financing go belly up. My suggestion is that until you've handled a few rental houses, hold up on tackling an apartment building. No, it's not impossible, but there are a few problems, including rent control.

The value of apartment buildings is directly related to their rental income. The higher the rental income, the greater the value. In the old days (meaning 20 years ago or more) the surest way to make money in real estate was to buy an apartment building, jack up the rents, and then resell. Typically for each dollar you increased your *annual* rental income you could get between $6 and $12 in profit on the sale. (If you had twenty units and raised the rent $25 on each, that meant an extra $500 a month, or $6000 a year, times a multiple of, for example, 9, meaning an instant profit of $54,000—all on a $25 rent increase.)

In most metropolitan areas, however, callous and unwarranted rent increases resulted in strict rent controls. Today if you have a building containing more than four units, in many if not most areas, you are limited in the rent increases you can make. Typically you must justify such increases dollar for dollar with your costs before you can impose them. Thus, your opportunity to raise the value of an apartment building is severely limited. As a result, during the last big price increases in real estate we saw single-family housing going up as much as 50 percent in value while many apartment buildings moved up only 5 to 7 percent.

Of course, there are still many areas without rent control. I have some friends who bought a twenty-two-unit apartment building in far northern California in a city without rent control. The place was run down and the rental income low because of poor paying tenants. They fixed up the property, rented aggressively, and resold in less than 18 months for triple their money, even in a cold market.

Single-Family Detached Houses

That leaves single-family detached houses (SFDH). I have heard experienced real estate investors, those who can afford to buy 100-unit apartment buildings, disparage the SFDH. I have heard them say, "If I have a hundred-unit building and I have one vacancy, it's only 1 percent of my income that I'm losing. But if you have a single-family house and have one vacancy, you lose 100 percent of your income. There's no way to justify that."

There is, of course. If you have one unit and find one tenant, you have 100 percent occupancy. If you have a 100-unit apartment, you have to find 100 tenants to get full occupancy.

Either way, it's just a war of words. What counts is results. I've been renting single-family housing for 30 years in good markets and bad and as long as I've been doing it *personally*, I've never had serious trouble finding a tenant. Oh, I might have to lower rents or offer enticements (such as a water allowance or a discount for rent paid on time) to get a good-paying tenant in a bad market. But I've always had my places full. (In 30 years I've never had a house vacant for more than 2 weeks, and that's a lot of houses.)

While you may not achieve that record, my feeling is that if you're new to investment real estate or if you want to expand, the place to expand initially is into single-family house. This area offers the best chance of finding tenants for the highest rent-to-cost ratios (the amount of rent produced for a given cost of purchasing the units).

Rule 3—Look for Strong
Tenant Markets

Real estate prices are falling, hence the rental market must be bad. Right? Think again. Except in a complete blow-out, the residential rental market often moves exactly *opposite* to the sales market. (*Note*: Here we are talking about single-family units, not necessarily condos, co-ops, or multiple units—although the markets for them are quite similar.)

The rationale is quite simple. When the market is strong, people tend to hang onto their real estate, particularly their rental real estate. Thus, there are a lot of units for rent, making the rental market soft.

On the other hand, when the housing market itself gets soft, people who have rentals often put them up for sale hoping to get their profits out before the market dips further. To get a buyer, they frequently keep their properties vacant. As a result, in a bad sales market there are actually fewer rental units and the rental market gets tighter.

You may not believe this is the case until you actually begin renting. Then you'll find that the divergence between the housing market and the rental market is quite striking, unless there is a blow-out. When the prices collapse, as they have done in Phoenix, both markets get soft as owners who find they can't sell their investment property try to rerent it.

Nevertheless, a cold real estate market often provides the best rental opportunities for landlords. Of course, there are the tenants to consider.

A Local Work Force

In order to get a tenant for your house, you must be able to draw on local workers. If there are no local jobs, you won't get any tenants.

It's important to do a tenant analysis before leaping ahead and buying rental property. There are a variety of ways to accomplish this and I'll list several of the simplest ones.

First, keep in mind that during a strong market it's generally considered an advantage to look for a blue-collar tenant. This person is likely to be consistently employed. However, in a cold market this person may be the first to be unemployed. In addition, blue-collar neighborhoods tend to be less expensive, but they also tend to become run down faster in a housing recession.

Thus, my suggestion is to look for a large body of white-collar workers in a medium-priced neighborhood. Check for office buildings, commercial buildings, industrial plants, financial institutions, and the like in your area.

Tip

Think like a tenant. If you're a tenant, who's going to employ you? Look around your area. Who are the big employers? Are they sound or in financial trouble? If sound and you were to work for them, where would you prefer to live (proximity, type of neighborhood, price, etc.). Find the place that the tenant wants to live and that's where you'll have your strongest tenant market.

Check the newspapers under "Houses for Rent." You'll see certain areas that have dozens of homes calling for tenants. Other areas, often with homes in same price range, may have only a few rentals. Recheck the paper over several weeks. You may find that the one area has the same homes advertised for weeks on end while the other finds tenants almost immediately.

The area which rents easily is a good rental market. The area with lots of vacancies is not.

Finally, you can check with brokers and rental agencies. Often in a single conversation they can give you as much information as you could collect in weeks of personally conducting your own investigations. (It's a good idea to do some personal leg work anyway, just to be sure that what you are being told is, in fact, accurate.)

Rule 4—Only Buy Property with a Good Price/Rent Ratio

Your strategy is to rent and hold. But in order to hold you have to be able to rent the property out for enough money to pay your expenses.

In truth these days it's probably impossible to rent a property for a complete break-even given the costs of finding tenants and of maintenance. But you should be able to rent it out at least for your principle, interest, taxes, and insurance (PITI). If you can cover the PITI, you can probably cover the maintenance and other costs by writing the depreciation off your personal income taxes. (*Note*: Recent tax law changes have severely limited a taxpayer's ability to deduct losses from "passive" investments, which real estate is usually considered. In Chapter 13 we will discuss exemptions to the rule for certain middle-income taxpayers.)

The price/rent ratio is simply a rule of thumb that wise investors use to gauge the relationship between monthly rental income, monthly expenses, and the price of the property. It simply says that the monthly income from rents should not be less than 1 percent of the total purchase price. If the monthly rent is less than 1 percent, the property is too expensive. Here's how to make the calculation:

$$\text{Ratio} = \frac{\text{purchase price}}{\text{monthly rent}}$$

If you divide the purchase price by the monthly rent, the resulting number should be 100 or lower. If it is, you have a favorable ratio. On the other hand, if the number is higher than 100, chances are you won't be able to make your monthly payments from the monthly rental income. This would result in your having to possibly take money out of your own pocket each month just to hang onto the property. Since you might need to hold the house for several years before the market turns around, this could amount to a substantial sum.

With a bad ratio, you're probably better off not buying the property, *even if otherwise it seems like a good deal.*

Tip

Because of the decline in housing values, the number of new housing units (homes, condos, apartments, etc.) has declined enormously. In other words, fewer residential units are being built. Given our increasing population, that means that there are going to be more people chasing fewer homes.

The result, inevitably, over the next few years is going to be higher rental rates. If you're really gutsy, you could buy a property with an un-favorable ratio, hoping to hold onto it until rental rates rise.

Of course, calculating the ratio is quite simple. The real trick is to determine what a house will rent for before you buy it. If the house is already rented, you can use that as your basis, maybe. (Be sure the house isn't rented to the owner's cousin for several hundred dollars higher than the going rental rate.)

Finding the Real Rental Rate

I'm a skeptic. I've been told I am and I believe it. The reason is that over time I've learned that most people will tell you what you want to hear and what benefits them. If you ask a broker or a seller what a house can be rented for, chances are you will be told that it can be rented for your PITI, whatever those costs may be.

Of course, the words may be hedged something like, "Well, if I were to rent it, I wouldn't ask for less than $ . . ." (fill in your PITI). The implication is that the seller or broker could get that amount. If, later on, you can't, the further implication is that there is something wrong with your rental abilities. As a result, I never rely on what anyone tells me with regard to the real rental income of a piece of property. I find out for myself.

Finding out the real rental rate isn't all that hard. You can do it in a few hours at most. Here's the procedure:

1. Categorize the house you are considering purchasing. On a sheet of paper list the following:

   Bedrooms

   Baths

   Special features (pool, fireplace, extra garage, etc.)

   Location

   This is all you basically need. Remember, tenants are not nearly as choosy as buyers. Tenants want a certain size home (number of bedrooms and baths), amenities (like a pool), and a certain location. Beyond that, assuming it's fairly clean and the price is right, they're ready to move in.

2. Check in the local newspaper for comparable rentals. Pick three, then call the owners and go look at them. Ask the landlords how long the properties have been for rent, is the landlord paying anything

extra (like utilities), what kind of security deposit and lease are required (month to month or leasehold), and the monthly rent.

3. Compare your notes. You should pretty quickly see what similar houses are renting for. Of course, you will want to recheck to see if these properties do, in fact, get rented. But if it turns out that homes similar to the one you are considering purchasing are renting, for example, for $900 a month, that's probably where your rental rate will realistically be.

Tip

Beware of a rental price resistance level. I have several homes in a bedroom community near Los Angeles. One is quite large (six bedrooms, four baths), the other is average (three bedrooms, two baths). In theory the larger house should rent for at least 50 percent more than the average-sized one. But it doesn't work out that way.

In this community there is a rental price resistance level of around $1100. Any three-bedroom, two-bath home ("3 + 2") will rent for at least $1100, which is what I rent my average-sized house out for. Tenants are readily available at this price. However, when I try to rent my larger house out for $1650 (roughly 1½ times $1100), it's much harder to find tenants. While on the average-sized house I might get four or five calls a day, on the large one I might get one or two calls a week.

In this particular community the price resistance level is at $1100 and renting above that range, though not impossible, is difficult. The result is that I can rent my average-priced home in a week. But it might take several months to rent the larger home at the higher rate. (I cut down that rental time to only a week or two by throwing in amenities such as gardener and pool service and by making sure the place is spotless before prospective tenants see it. I'm sure to get those one or two higher-paying tenants who are available before any other landlord does.)

Rule 5—Know What Your Expenses Will Be

We've just looked at how to determine your rental income (Rule 4). Now we need to turn our attention toward determining what you can expect in rental expenses. (Without knowing your true expenses, purchasing an investment property would be a real crap shoot. You might come out okay—and then, on the other hand, you might jump into a real disaster.)

We've already touched on the three fixed expenses that you will incur:

Mortgage payments (could be a variable if you have an adjustable rate mortgage; see Chapter 11)

Taxes

Insurance

In addition there are several other variable expenses. By the way, "variable" does not mean that you may or may not incur them. It means that while they will definitely be there, the amounts will vary month to month and year to year.

Maintenance

The biggest variable expense is maintenance. Maintenance is an unknown factor. You won't know what's going to break until it does. However, depending on the age of the property, here are some pretty good guesses:

Typical Maintenance Items and Costs*

Item	Cost	Frequency
Water heater	$300	6–9 years
Carpeting	?†	3–7 years
Furnace	$1500	15 years
Air conditioner	$300–1500	3–10 years
Garbage disposal	$150	5 years
Washer and dryer	$300 (each)	7 years
Refrigerator	$600	15 years
Faucet washers	$50 (plumber)	6 months
Stove/oven	$400	5–10 years
Roof	$3000–7000	15–20 years
Painting inside	$500–1000	3–4 years
Painting outside	$1500	5–7 years
Door locks	$35 apiece	Every new tenancy
Plumbing repairs	$200–$500	Annually
Electrical repairs	$50	Annually
Landscaping	$500–$1500	Annually
Gardener	$1500	Annually
Pool service	$1000	Annually

*Note: Costs are as of this writing. They are sure to increase over time.

†Carpeting costs vary enormously. As of this writing they are a *minimum* of about $15 to $20 a yard (a yard is 9 square feet).

The above list is not set in stone. Obviously if you don't have a pool, you won't have pool service. And if the house is under 7 years old, you won't have many of the other items such as a new water heater or roof. But over time, you will probably experience the need to pay for more items on the list than you might anticipate.

I've been asked on many an occasion what a typical annual maintenance for a house might be. Of course, it's impossible to give a truly accurate figure. However, I think the following list suggests what you might expect to pay, on average, each year depending on the age of the property:

Typical Annual Maintenance Costs

Age	Cost*
Under 7 years old	$1500
7 to 20 years old	$2000
21 years and older	$3000

*Excluding gardener and pool service.

If you buy a brand new house, there will undoubtedly be many additional thousands of dollars of expenses in putting in landscaping and fencing.

Your Time

Finally, there is the matter of your time. Most new and small investors in real estate deeply discount their time. They tend to figure that it's spare time anyhow, so what's the difference?

The point, of course, is what is called "substitution" in economics. If you weren't out fixing a leaky faucet in your rental, you could be earning money at a second job (or first job) or staying home watching the 49ers battle the Broncos on TV. In order to calculate the value of your time, you have to *substitute* what you might otherwise be doing with that time.

The best way of handling substitution that I know of is to figure an hourly wage for yourself. What is it worth to you, per hour, to be working on a rental property?

Some people calculate their hourly wage at their regular work rate. Others figure what it would cost if they hired someone to do the job (like a plumber or electrician). Still others figure it's mostly spare time so they just figure in the minimum wage.

It really doesn't matter how you calculate it. The point is that you need to figure that your time is worth something. To see why, let's take a hypothetical figure. We'll just assume that your time is worth $10 an hour. (It's probably worth a whole lot more, but remember, this is just an illustration.) Let's further suppose that you'll need to find a tenant at least once a year and that you'll make a dozen separate trips to the house over that year to collect the rent, fix a faucet or sprinkler head, or to make some other minor repair.

Typical Landlord's Time Costs

Activity	Time (hours)
Finding a tenant (including placing ads in newspaper, talking to prospective tenants on the phone, showing the property and staying at home by the phone waiting for prospective tenants to call)	75
12 trips to property (assuming 30 minutes each way and an hour there each time)	36
Keeping records and working with an accountant, CPA, or tax attorney	10
Total	121

Thus, 121 hours @ $10 hourly = $1210 annually. In other words, you can figure that it's going to cost you roughly $100 a month of your time for the rental, assuming you are only worth $10 an hour. If, on the other hand, you're a professional who makes $100 an hour, it will cost you $1000 a month of your time to take care of the property.

As I mentioned earlier, these maintenance and personal operating costs are rarely, if ever, covered by the rental income (which goes to pay PITI). As a consequence, they are out-of-pocket costs that you must pay and then add to your total costs for buying and holding the property.

Of course, you can deduct the actual maintenance costs (not your personal time, however) on the property from your income taxes. You may also be able to deduct depreciation, depending on your financial situation (see Chapter 13). But even if you do, under current tax laws (no capital gains), when you sell the property, your depreciation will come back at you as regular income.

Vacancies

No property is rented all of the time. If you're a good landlord and on top of things, however, it can be rented most of the time. A good rule of thumb for a good landlord to use is that the property will be vacant at least 2 weeks out of each year. (Assuming you've picked a strong rental market and that you actively participate in getting tenants.)

Rule 6—Get Favorable Terms

Sellers are typically hung up on price. Even in a declining market, even after they've lowered their price 10 or 15 percent, many sellers would rather lose a sale than lower it an additional 1 or 2 percent. They are convinced that lowering price is the absolute last resort.

The problem for sellers, of course, is that the market for their home may be far lower than the price they are asking. For example, Dorothy wanted to sell her home for $200,000. This was close to the highest price anyone had ever gotten for a similar home in her neighborhood (in a sale nearly a year earlier.)

Dorothy listed her house for $200,000. When she had no offers, she dropped it 5 percent to $190,000. Then another 5 percent to $180,000. At this point she balked. She told her broker she would rather not sell than lower it any further. Her broker told her, however, that the current market price for homes like hers in her neighborhood was around $165,000. She was wasting her time at the $180,000 price. Dorothy wouldn't budge.

At this point an investor entered the picture and decided that Dorothy's house would be a good property to buy. He felt that $165,000 was a fair price. But when the agent disclosed that Dorothy was firm at $180,000, the investor paused. He could, of course, make the low-ball offer and very likely Dorothy would refuse.

His quandary was this, how could he get Dorothy to accept a realistic value when she was hung up on price? He considered. Perhaps by obtaining favorable terms he could transform a high value into a low one all the while placating Dorothy by giving her the $180,000 that she wanted. Here's how he did it.

The then current interest rate was 12 percent. What if he asked Dorothy to carry back paper (financing) at, for example, 7 percent. How much of a difference would that make to him? He planned to hold the house 5 years. Could the difference in interest rates make up for $15,000 difference between the true market value and the price Dorothy was asking?

The Deal at $180,000 and 7 Percent Financing

Dorothy owed about $60,000 on the house, so he would definitely need to get a new loan for that amount. That left $120,000. If he put 10 percent down, or $18,000, it would leave a balance of $102,000. What would the interest he would have to pay on that money be over 5 years?

$60,000 mortgage at 12 percent	$36,000
$102,000 mortgage at 7 percent	$35,700
Total interest	$71,700 (paid over 5 years)

The Deal at $165,000 and 12 Percent Financing

On the other hand, how would the deal come out if he got the lower price and paid the higher rate of interest? At $165,000 the investor would have to put only $16,500 ($1500 less) down and would get a new loan for roughly $148,500 at 12 percent. The total 5-year interest would be:

$148,500 mortgage at 12 percent	$89,100 (paid over 5 years)

The Savings in *interest only* by Offering a Higher Price, but Getting Better Financing

$165,000 and 12 percent financing	$89,100
$180,000 and 7 percent financing	$71,700
Total interest savings	$17,400
Less the extra down payment at the higher price	$ 1,500
Total 5-year interest savings	$15,900

In other words by offering the Dorothy full price and better terms, over 5 years the investor would actually save $15,900 in interest. Since the higher price was only $15,000 more than the actual market value of the property, that's a net savings to the investor of about $900. In other words, because of the difference in terms, from the investor's perspective, it was cheaper to offer a higher price and better terms than a low-ball price and standard terms.

Of course, things won't always work out this neatly. But, I believe the point is made. Terms are critical. Often you can give the seller his or her price and still get a bargain by negotiating for more favorable terms for yourself.

Rule 7—Be Sure that You Get a Bargain Price and Not an Inflated Value

In the previous example we saw how terms could be manipulated to make a high price into a low one. The point now is that no matter what the effective price you get, you want to be sure that it's at or below market.

The real question, therefore, becomes how to determine market price. We'll look at this from two perspectives. The first is by considering the market itself. The second by considering the seller.

Bargain Prices at the Market

In a rising real estate market, judging market price is fairly easy to do. Comparables are your biggest help. Typically houses are selling rapidly and there are many sales of homes in neighborhoods similar to the one in which you are considering buying. You can look at comparables and see what price houses recently have been selling for. Perhaps (in a rising market) you will add a little on to the price for appreciation when you make your offer.

In a falling market it's quite different. Typically there are far fewer sales. (If sales were plentiful, the market wouldn't be falling.) Additionally, those sales which have been made, going back 6 months or more, may often reflect a higher price than the current market warrants. Thus, comparables are not nearly as good a guide.

In a sluggish market comparables should be used to gauge where the market was 3 to 6 months (or more) ago. Once you establish that figure, you have to determine how much the market has fallen, if any, since then.

This is strictly a judgment call. But, there are lots of clues to help you along the way. For one thing, check monthly average and median prices of recent home sales (available from brokers). These will help give you a picture of what the market's doing now. For another, check inventories. Figure 3-1 showed the bell-shaped curve the housing inventories take during a falling market. Check to see where you are on the curve. If inventories of unsold homes are continuing to rise month to month, the market is still falling. If, on the other hand, inventories have leveled off or even begun to recede (accompanied by firming prices), it's a good clue that the market has bottomed out.

Tip

In a falling market there is no way to know what a good price for a home really is. The reason, simply, is that any price you assign today may become too high as the market falls tomorrow. If you find that you are in a falling market, my suggestion is to back off and wait. Wait until you are sure the market has bottomed.

Trap

Beware of blow-outs. As noted in several areas of this book, blow-outs have occurred in Arizona, Texas, and parts of the northeast as well in the oil patch states and the Midwest earlier in the last decade.

A blow-out is when prices free-fall because of the number of houses put onto the market and the lack of buyers. You will be able to tell a blow-out by the newspaper articles bemoaning the sad real estate market, by the vast numbers of sellers trying to dump their houses at any price, and by the accompanying bad rental market. (As noted earlier in this chapter, in a simple slump, the rental market moves opposite to the real estate sales market—sales prices drop while rental prices tend to hold steady or increase. In a blow-out they move together—sales prices as well as rental prices decline.) Buying into a blow-out is the kiss of death. You are sure to pay too much.

If the market has bottomed out, it's time to think about investing. However, you're still faced with determining market value. As noted, comparables are most likely based on sales of 6 months or more ago and, hence, may suggest prices that are too high. What are you to do?

Making Low-Ball Offers

My suggestion is that you only low-ball sellers. This is a technique that some investors have worked out to perfection. It requires two elements: persistence and guts.

The persistence is required by the fact that you won't get a seller to accept every time or every other time or even every fifth or perhaps tenth time. You have to be willing to make offers that get turned down time and again. You have to be willing to keep on trying until you finally hit the right seller.

Trap

Don't fall in love with an investment house. When you buy a house to live in, you're allowed to fall in love with it. When you buy to invest, you're not. An investment house is strictly a business proposition. One house is as good as another and you simply want one that will meet your financial and economic criteria. Never mind the cute archway in the living room or the adorable French windows. The questions you need to ask have to do with price, terms, rentability, and ultimate resale. Leave your heart home when buy investment property. Bring only your head.

Guts come in because you have to be willing to accept a lot of criticism. Real estate brokers will criticize your actions. (This is only natural since, in most cases, they represent sellers and since they don't get paid a commission unless there's a sale. They don't like making lots of unsuccessful offers.)

You also have to have the courage to try and try again even after many offers are rejected. Remember, you want and need to buy at the bottom of the market. Helping a poor seller out of the difficult situation he or she got into is not your responsibility. Your goal is to get a good deal.

Tip

Normally a buyer will come back with a counteroffer. However, if you've really low-balled, that counteroffer often will still be tens of thousands of dollars too high. You have to be prepared to stick to your original offer (or come up just a bit). In short, you have to be prepared to walk away if you don't get the deal that you want.

How Low Is Low?

When you don't know how low to make an offer, what should you do? My suggestion is to start at the comparables and find the last similar houses that sold. Next check the inventories to see when the market bottomed out. If the bottom was at or before the last comparable sales, those figures may be quite accurate.

If the market bottomed out some time after those comparables were sold, consider offering between *½ to 1 percent per month* lower than the asking price for each month between the time the comparable sales were made and the time the market bottomed.

For example, let's say the comparables are 8 months old and the market bottomed out 3 months ago. That means it was falling for 5 months after the comparable sales. Consider offering between 2½ and 5 percent below the *lowest* comparable sales price.

Once again, remember that this is only a rule of thumb. You may want to drop the price considerably more depending on the attitude of the seller. In the next chapter we'll go into seller's attitudes in far more detail.

The Seven Rules

1. Never look far from home
2. Buy single-family housing
3. Look for strong tenant markets
4. Only buy property with a good price/rent ratio
5. Know what your expenses will be
6. Get favorable terms
7. Be sure that you get a bargain price and not an inflated value

These, then, are the seven rules for buying right. No, they won't guarantee success. But follow them and they will put you head and shoulders ahead of other investors who don't.

6

Finding Motivated Sellers

Not long ago I was talking with an Arizona investor, Kerry, who had purchased a property in Phoenix for $10 down, cash. That's right, the full down payment (including closing costs) was $10.

Naturally enough I asked Kerry how she had managed to structure the deal. It was simple, she pointed out. She had run into a seller who was desperate to sell. This seller, Ernest, lived in California, yet his investment house was in Arizona. Because of the poor market, Ernest couldn't get rid of the house no matter what he did.

Ernest had originally paid close to $60,000 for the property. Now it was worth closer to $35,000. It turned out that he had an assumable (the debt could be assumed by a new buyer without penalty) FHA loan on the house. When Kerry ran into him, the house had not produced income for over a year. Oh, he had rented it several times during that period through property managers. But, the tenants had either skipped without paying the rent or in one case had stayed and had to be evicted. The house was costing Ernest about $600 a month out of his pocket, every month.

When he tried to sell, he learned it was a blown out market. Tens of thousands of homes were for sale and there were few buyers. He had listed it for 6 months and during that time had received no offers.

Ernest was at the end of his rope. He couldn't afford to keep making the $600 a month payments. Yet, he couldn't sell. He had decided that the only solution was to let the lender take the property back through foreclosure. The problem there, of course, was that would ruin his credit.

Kerry says she met Ernest on a flight to Los Angeles from Phoenix. He was returning after flying to his house to repaint the outside himself (to save money) after vandals had sprayed graffiti all over it. Kerry and Ernest struck up a conversation and she had agreed to look at the property upon her return.

Kerry said that because she lived in Phoenix, she could oversee the property with ease. She could find the right tenant and rent it out for the mortgage payments, taxes, and insurance. It would be a good investment for her. But, there were so many properties available that she saw no advantage in putting any money into this one. The only way it was better than others was if she could get it for nothing down. So she called Ernest and offered him $10. Ernest was to pay the modest closing costs. (They ran no escrow and had no title insurance—Kerry simply did a title search. She wasn't worried about a bad title, however, since she was putting virtually nothing into the property.)

Ernest, on the other hand, was thrilled. The day before he had been looking at foreclosure and the ruination of his credit. Now, Kerry was bailing him out. He grabbed at the chance to get out of the property.

This true story illustrates the kind of desperate seller that you should be looking for when you search for bargain properties. The seller's motivation may be different, but the motivation must be there.

One other important point to note is that this was a "win-win" deal. Kerry won by getting a house for next to nothing. But the seller, Ernest, also won by saving his credit reputation. If Kerry hadn't come along, he would have had a foreclosure to his name.

Judging the Seller

In the last chapter, we said that half the battle in finding bargain property is judging the market. The other half (and some say the bigger half) is judging the seller. In today's market you not only have to know what the realistic price is for a property, you have to find a seller who is motivated enough to accept that price.

Remember, most sellers of single-family homes have the option of withdrawing their homes from the market if they don't get their price. Most sellers are *not* desperate. They have the option of deferring a move to another home.

Tip

Typically most sellers visualize their price as what a comparable house sold for when the market was last hot. For example, the seller may well be aware that a year and a half ago a house just like his or hers sold for $200,000. Today the market may be at $140,000. But the seller doesn't want to recognize the reality of today's market. Rather he or she wants to get that $200,000 price of yesterday. When that price can't be achieved, most sellers withdraw the house from sale and do just what you want to do—hold onto it until prices turn around.

Thus, in order for you to get a bargain price you need to find a seller who must sell. There are at least six good reasons a seller must sell and you need to find one who is being pressured by one of the following:

1. There is a *job change* to a different area, necessitating a move.
2. The seller has *bought another home* and has to sell this one in order to close the deal on the next.
3. The seller has *lost his or her job* or for other reasons is in financial difficulty and needs to get out quickly.
4. The seller *wants to "move up"* to a bigger house or to a better area (this is a low motivation).
5. The seller has some *other problems* such as a divorce and simply must get rid of the house immediately.
6. For one reason or another the seller *can't make the payments* on the property and must sell or lose it.

In each of the above cases the seller must get out. He or she will be willing to accept a realistic price (or offer better terms—see the last chapter) because of that motivation. Unless the seller has one of the above motivations (or one of similar intensity), your chances of getting the house at a realistic price may be just about nil. Without motivation the seller will simply take the property off the market and sit on it.

How to Find Out the Seller's Motivation

How do you find out what the seller's motivation really is? It's a cardinal rule in selling real estate that as a seller you always keep up the best front. That's the way to get your price. If you let a potential buyer know you're desperate, you'll get a lower offer. So, how do you, as a buyer, find out which sellers are desperate? The answer is simple. Desperate sellers always tell you they are desperate.

Why would a seller break the cardinal rule? The reason is that desperate sellers want out, now. They realize that it's no longer a matter of getting the best price; they want any price. They want to sell. Keeping their desperation to themselves won't do the trick. The only way they can get out is if they let every potential buyer, everyone who is even remotely a potential buyer, know their situation. (That's why Ernest initially told Kerry his situation on their flight.)

As a result, it's not a secret. If the house is listed, ask the real estate broker. A desperate seller will instruct the broker to "Find any buyer. Tell them that I'm desperate. Get me an offer."

Check with Brokers

The real estate broker will move on these words. Any agent worth his or her salt knows that a desperate seller means a quick sale. The broker will alert every potential buyer, including you, that this seller wants out.

Consequently, your first source of desperate buyers is the real estate broker.

Tip

As an investment buyer, it's a good idea to work with many brokers. While it is true that most homes which are listed appear on the multiple listing service, not all do. Sometimes a broker will take a listing which he or she feels is such a bargain that it will sell without being "co-broked." They will keep it for themselves.

It's a good idea, therefore, to get friendly with half a dozen agents in the area's most active offices. Let them know what you are looking for and that you are ready to act, if and when they come up with the right property. You can be sure they will call you first thing if something good shows up.

Note: Don't worry about agents buying a bargain themselves before letting you know about it. Nearly all agents depend on getting commissions from sales for their livelihood. It is the rare agent who will have the means or the incentive to buy a property him or herself, rather than make a quick sale and collect a commission on it.

Check with Sellers

Another good way to find out a seller's motivation is to ask the seller. It's really quite simple. Very frequently when you look at a house, the seller will be there. Just begin a conversation and ask why that seller wants to sell. If they hedge and haw or give a reason that is not indicative of strong motivation, pass. On the other hand the motivated seller is very likely to simply let you know that they are extremely eager to get a deal. They may say something like, "Make me an offer." Or, "Let's talk. If you're interested, put it in writing. I'm very anxious to get out of here." Motivated sellers will seldom try to hide their eagerness. Rather, they will do everything to let you know just how they feel.

Check with Neighbors

Ask around. Oftentimes neighbors are excellent sources of information. And neighbors may feel little loyalty to the existing owner who is selling and leaving the neighborhood.

Of course, this is not an invitation to be a snoop or to invade anyone's privacy. However, I always suggest that anyone who is interested in buying a property should always talk to the neighbors, first. (It's a lot easier on the nervous system to learn there is a bad neighbor next door before you buy than after.) As part of your conversation with the neighbor, you will certainly ask about the house, the neighborhood, and eventually the conversation will drift over to the seller. The neighbor may volunteer some critical information about why the seller is getting out.

Desperate Sellers in Foreclosure

Thus far, we've been assuming that we will find motivated sellers who have their homes listed for sale. But what about sellers who haven't been able to sell their homes for one reason or another and are now in foreclosure? They are the most desperate of all to sell and they, on occasion, may be able to present some terrific bargain opportunities to you. How do we find these?

It's important to understand how foreclosure works. It's somewhat different state by state, but the process overall is much the same in most areas of the country. There are essentially three stages:

1. The seller can't or won't make payments and the lender puts the mortgage in default.

2. After a legally determined period of time the lender "sells" the property to the highest bidder "on the court house steps."

3. Typically the lender is the highest bidder. It takes control of the property and now attempts to resell it as a real estate owned (REO) property. This will be discussed in Chapter 8.

What we're concerned with here is stage 1. The seller can't or won't make payments. He or she is desperate to sell the property, hoping to recoup any equity at the most and save his or her credit rating at the least. This seller is going to listen to any offer that you make.

How to Find Sellers Who Are in Foreclosure

In a cold real estate market there are far more sellers in foreclosure than you might imagine. A motivated seller who can't find a buyer can rapidly turn into a desperate seller who can't make the payments and who is facing the loss of the property. The big question becomes, how do you locate this person?

FSBOS.   One method is to look for sale by owner signs (FSBOS). Typically this person has made many efforts to liquidate the property. They may have had it listed, but the listing expired with no results. Now facing foreclosure, they may feel they can't afford to pay a commission. Hence, they are trying to sell it themselves. Typically such efforts are relatively nonproductive and as the house moves into foreclosure may be done halfheartedly. In fact the only efforts may be a sign in the front yard that says, "For Sale by Owner."

Once you've determined where you want to buy your investment house, begin touring the area. Drive up and down the streets. Chances are you'll run into an occasional FSBO. Stop, introduce yourself, and talk to the seller. It will most often be that the seller really is only trying to sell FSBO in order to save paying a commission. When this doesn't work (it doesn't in 99 percent of the cases), the seller will list with an agent. However, occasionally you will find someone who is in foreclosure. When you do, you've got your motivated seller.

Agents.   Agents will also know if any of their sellers are in foreclosure. However, the opportunity to pick up a bargain may be diminished here. If you buy, you will have to come up with enough money to pay the agent's commission plus back payments and penalties on the mortgage. It won't be a clean deal with you buying the property "for $10 down" as did Kerry in our opening example.

Title Insurance and Trust Companies.   This is useful in states which use the "trust deed" device instead of the older "mortgage." (Currently over 40 states use the trust deed as the preferred lending device.)

In a traditional mortgage there are two parties—the borrower and the lender. To foreclose the lender must begin legal proceedings in court. With a trust deed, however, there are three parties. The borrower (trustor), the lender (beneficiary), and the trustee. When the lender loans to the borrower the money on the house, the borrower gives to the trustee the right to sell that house if he or she doesn't keep up the payments. The trustee, in short, holds the potential power to sell the property.

When the borrower doesn't pay, the lender notifies the trustee that the borrower is in default and the trustee begins foreclosure proceedings. The time period for this varies from state to state from as long as about 4 months (in states such as California) to a very short 30-day period (in states such as Texas.) (The trust deed is preferred because of the relatively short time involved in foreclosure. Judicial foreclosure of a mortgage can take years. In addition, with judicial foreclosure there is a redemption period during which the former owner can reclaim the property by repaying the debt, penalties, and costs. With a trust deed foreclosure there is typically no redemption period after the sale.)

Now, here's the important part with regard to finding properties in trust deed foreclosure. The trustee named in the trust deed is typically a title insurance and trust company. These companies are set up to handle the position of trustee and to handle foreclosures, which is why they are so named by most lenders.

Hence, if you become known to a title insurance and trust company, they may be willing to let you have a list of properties they have in foreclosure. They do not widely advertise or disseminate such lists but instead make them available to their clients and "friends." (A goodly number of investors have gotten rich in the past simply by becoming fast friends with a title insurance company officer.)

Legal Papers. Of course, there's nothing secret about such a list. It's just more convenient to get it from a title insurance company. If you can't, however, there is another alternative. The first step in foreclosure is the filing of a notice of default. This notice usually must be filed with the county recorder's office. (This applies to mortgages as well as trust deeds.) You could always spend some time at the county recorder's office checking for notices of default that have been filed. Few of us, however, have such time to spend.

Another alternative may be to check the "legal newspaper" in your area. Most larger areas will have a newspaper whose sole purpose is to carry legal notices. If you've only subscribed to the larger consumer newspapers, you may have never heard of it. But a call to any title insurance company officer or the county clerk's office will confirm its existence and probably get you a number to call.

The legal newspapers are filled with legal notices such as doing business under a fictitious name ("dba") notifications or other items that people are legally required to publish. In addition they often publish such items as notices of default.

Of course, one of the problems with checking these notices (as well as the notices filed with the county clerk) is that they tend to give the "legal description" of the property. Instead of 32 Maple Street they may give a tract, block, and map number. Unless you're able to read recorded maps, such information isn't all that helpful.

Which brings us to the final source. Usually advertised in legal newspapers are private listing companies which, for a fee, will sell you a list of properties in foreclosure that gives their common street address. Be aware, however, that this list is frequently costly, often more than a hundred dollars a month. (Which is why it's nice to have a friend at a title insurance company who will give you such a list free.) Just call up and subscribe as you would to any other service.

Lenders.   This is a very difficult alternative to use, but when you can, it is probably the best way to learn of properties in foreclosure. Usually in any given area there are one or two large savings and loans or banks which handle a large percentage of the mortgages. These lenders, consequently, also end up taking back most of the properties that go into foreclosure.

Each S&L has a foreclosure department (not to be confused with an REO department, discussed separately). The foreclosure department handles delinquent mortgages. Most S&Ls are reluctant to release such lists, for reasons discussed shortly. But, having a friend in such a department who is willing to share the S&L's list with you can prove to be very profitable.

Dealing with an Owner in Foreclosure

Once you find someone who is in foreclosure, it's now up to you to contact them directly and find out if there is a good deal available for you. You should already have a name and an address and possibly even a phone number. Now, just give this person a call. Explain that you're an investor and that you're looking for property in the area. You heard they were having some difficulty in making payments and you're wondering if there's a way to make a win-win situation out of it—they get their credit saved (plus, perhaps some money depending on their equity) and you get the property.

Be forewarned. Some people won't want to talk with you. They may be nasty, even offensive. They usually take their foreclosure personally and may blame everyone but themselves for it. Forget them. They can't be helped and most likely will lose their house and their credit.

Others will be happy, even eager to talk. Those are the ones you want to work with. When you find such an owner, you have to determine what it's going to cost you to take over the property.

Costs of Righting a Foreclosure

What you can offer to the owner is to make up the back payments and penalties and save the owner's credit rating in exchange for the title to the property. In other words, you can offer to take it over. The advantage here is that, like Kerry in our first example, you get the property for virtually no money down. The disadvantage is that the loan may not be assumable. You may not only have to make up back payments and penalties but also secure a new loan with accompanying points and fees.

In short, it may cost you many thousands of dollars to take over this property and bail out this owner. You may find that by the time you add up the costs, it simply isn't worthwhile. The following are some potential costs involved in righting a foreclosure:

1. Back payments (Could be as much as 6 months of payments or more.)
2. Penalties (Each month that the payment is late usually incurs a penalty. In addition there may be additional penalties as time periods in the foreclosure process expire.)
3. New loan costs including points, fees, title insurance, etc. (Typically this will be about 5 percent of the loan amount—on a $100,000 mortgage figure about $5000.)
4. Fixing up the property (The former owner may not have kept the place in great shape once he or she learned they were going to lose it. You could have to spend several thousand in refurbishing and relandscaping.)

It's important that you calculate these costs as accurately as possible *before* you make any kind of offer to the owner. You may find that it simply isn't worth your time to attempt to right the foreclosure and take over the property. Here's an example of how this might happen.

Sandy's House. Leonard bought his southern California home in 1988, right at the height of the last boom in prices. He paid $300,000 for it, a typical price for the area. He put 20 percent down, or $60,000, and took out a $240,000 mortgage.

Everything seemed rosy until Leonard, a defense industry worker, was laid off. Suddenly he found he could not make his monthly payments. He immediately put his house up for sale asking $325,000. (The $25,000 above his purchase price was to make up for the commission and other costs involved in the sale. He really only wanted the $60,000 out that he had originally put in.)

A sale at that price, however, was out of the question. Real estate had gone down hill and prices had fallen in the local market. He had no takers at $325,000. He had no takers when he lowered his price to $300,000 or even $280,000. At that point he had used up his savings and could no longer make the monthly payments.

The listing had also expired and Leonard, angry at the broker for not bringing in any buyers, decided to try to sell for himself and, at the least, save the commission. Sandy came along about this time.

Sandy was an investor who was "bottom fishing." She was looking for bargain properties in a depressed market. Leonard's name had popped up on a list of properties in foreclosure and she gave him a call. He seemed eager and enthusiastic so she went to see him.

The property was in a good tenant market and Leonard was certainly a motivated seller. So Sandy was excited about the prospects and began to figure out the costs involved, which were:

3 month's back payments	$ 7,500
Penalties	400
Fixing up house	1,100
Securing new loan	12,000 (Leonard's old loan was not assumable)
Total costs	21,000

It would cost Sandy roughly $21,000 to pay off Leonard's existing loan (including back payments and penalties) and other costs. At that time Sandy calculated the market value of the house was roughly $260,000. Leonard still owed $240,000 (the payback of principle in the first years of a mortgage are virtually nil). This was a fixed figure. Leonard could not sell it for less than he owed.

The bottom line was that if Sandy were to take over the property it would cost her about $1000 more than the house was actually worth. So she made this offer to Leonard. She would save his credit, by paying off his existing mortgage that was in default, and would take over the house putting a new mortgage on it.

Leonard was ecstatic. That was exactly what he wanted. He said that he was glad to see that someone as bright and as honest as Sandy had finally come along. And to make sure that she knew how much she was appreciated, he was willing to accept a lower payment for his equity, say $50,000 for the $60,000 he had originally put up.

This was the hard part for Sandy. She swallowed and then explained the hard facts to Leonard.

It didn't make any difference what he had paid. It didn't make any different how much or how little he put into the property. The only thing that mattered was today's market value and today's costs.

She carefully showed him how her market analysis as well as her analysis of comparables in the area pointed to the fact that his house was worth only $260,000. She commiserated with him over the fact that the money he had put up only 18 months earlier was now simply gone. Finally, she carefully showed him her analysis of how much it would cost her to correct the default and to get a new loan (since his was not assumable).

Finally, she noted that her costs were $1000 more than the true equity he had in the property. The bottom line for Leonard was that if he wanted Sandy to bail out his credit, he would have to come up with a $1000 to pay her.

Leonard was aghast. He ranted and raved and finally asked her to leave, making it clear that he thought she was some sort of low-life who was taking advantage of the financial plight of poor individuals who had fallen on hard times.

To no avail did Sandy attempt to point out that the current market collapse and Leonard's financial woes were none of her doing. He would not listen to her explanation of the realities of the current market place. And he grew angry when she pointed out that she was offering him a real benefit, the saving of his credit. (With a foreclosure against him he would have trouble qualifying for any new mortgage and most credit for many years to come.)

Leonard wouldn't listen. So Sandy left and began looking for another investment house. Two weeks later Leonard called. He had thought it over. He still didn't like Sandy's deal and he was still fairly sure there was some crookedness in it somewhere. But he had talked to several other people and the importance of his good credit had been pointed out to him. So he agreed to accept Sandy's offer.

Unfortunately, during those 2 weeks there was additional interest and penalties on his mortgage so he ultimately had to pay Sandy $2500 to take over his property. Never the less, he walked away unburdened and with relatively clean credit. (His credit still showed late payments—but there was no foreclosure against it.)

It's important to point out that Sandy had to come up with a 10 percent down payment, or $26,000, and get a new loan for $234,000 with hefty payments to boot. But she was in a great tenant area and was able to rent the property out. And she bought it at bottom-of-the-market price so it was a good, albeit expensive deal for her.

Trap

The above example illustrates a win-win situation. However, some un-scrupulous fortune hunters have taken advantage of sellers who were financially pressed and mentally distressed by their pending foreclosure. In our above example, Leonard really had no equity, given the costs of saving his house. However, if he had bought earlier, he might have had a far lower loan and much greater equity. These fortune hunters, however, have offered such sellers essentially the same deal, reaping the benefits of the owner's greater equity.

As a result, many states have enacted laws protecting those in foreclosure from being preyed upon by fortune hunters. Typically such laws allow a certain period of time for recision of a sales agreement when the seller is in default on a mortgage. The period of time can vary from a few days to as long as 6 months or more after the sale.

If you buy the house unaware of these protective laws and the market suddenly turns around, you may find the original seller coming back and demanding those profits. Before you attempt to buy a home from a seller who is in foreclosure, check with a good real estate attorney in your state, who can give you correct information and forms to have the seller sign to help avoid having sellers later rescind sales agreements.

(Note: This particular right of recision does not apply to the lender who originally gave the mortgage. Usually, but not always, if you buy the property from the lender, you don't have to worry about the original owner coming back at you.)

Advantages of Dealing with Owners in Foreclosure

The obvious advantage of dealing with an owner in foreclosure is that you can get a property at the right price for the current market. If the house happens to be run down and in need of repair, you may get a price far below market. In short, dealing with owners in foreclosure is a way of finding bargain properties.

Buying at Foreclosure Sales

Another way of purchasing a property is by actually buying it when it is sold on the courthouse steps. At the time of foreclosure sale, the lender always offers the full price of the mortgage (or trust deed). But there is nothing to prevent you or anyone else from offering more.

Your offer, however, must be in the form of cash, so you will have to work out financing in advance. And you will receive no title insurance or other guarantees as to the status of the property. (You might, for example, think you're bidding on a first mortgage only to find that it's a second or third. This could be a catastrophe for you.)

It is beyond the scope of this book to go into detail on buying homes at foreclosure auctions. This is usually in the venue of attorneys and those well versed in real estate practice and law. It can also be a highly profitable area. If you are interested in it, you might consider consulting with a real estate attorney in your area who specializes in the field.

Buying Property in Foreclosure

As we've seen, it's not easy, but it does work. And it does highlight the theme of this chapter—getting a realistic price by finding motivated sellers. In Chapter 8 we'll go into finding properties in the final stage of foreclosure, when they are REOs offered by lenders.

7

Working with the Resolution Trust Corporation

RTC stands for Resolution Trust Corporation. The RTC was created by the federal government as part of the bail out of the savings and loan industry. Its purpose is to dispose of properties that the government obtained when it took over failed S&Ls.

The number of RTC properties varies from time to time. Estimates are, however, that the Corporation will be selling several hundred thousand properties well into 1993 and beyond. As of this writing the RTC has over 35,000 properties in its current inventory.

While relatively few of the properties handled by the RTC are single-family residences, they are located in every state although the vast majority happen to be in Texas. Some states, such as California, have almost none.

The RTC holds property under two categories—conservatorship and receivership. When an institution, such as an S&L, is determined to be insolvent, it is placed under the control of the RTC and becomes a "conservatorship institution." Foreclosed properties of the S&L come under control of the RTC. Properties in the foreclosure process or those which are deemed to be needing foreclosure are likewise controlled by the RTC.

Eventually the RTC may be able to sell the institution to a solvent S&L, to another organization, or even to an independent investor. The new owner typically takes over many but not all of the assets of the old and insolvent S&L. Those properties which do not go to the new owner are retained as a receivership asset.

The reason it's important to know the difference between conservatorship and receivership properties is that the first are sold by the original institution, under the auspices of the RTC. The second are sold directly by the RTC. Some differences sometimes do occur in the procedure for buying from the institution versus buying direct from the RTC.

Why Would You Be Interested in an RTC Property?

At the turn of the last decade there were hundreds of savings and loan institutions which failed. The causes of the failure are of little concern to us here except to note that in most cases they came about because of poor lending practices. The institutions gave mortgages to borrowers who were not really qualified or on property that wasn't worth what appraisers said it was—or both.

When the borrowers couldn't make the payments, the S&Ls instituted foreclosure proceedings. Having too much foreclosed property, ultimately, contributed to the demise of most of the S&Ls.

When the S&Ls were determined to be insolvent and the RTC took over the properties, it had to sell the properties. It is at this juncture that the opportunity for you comes into play.

Typically the properties that the S&L took back were overappraised. That means that the appraised value that was originally placed on them was based on the inflated prices of the last real estate boom. (Many were based on anticipated future inflated prices, which was even worse.)

When these were taken back, the S&Ls tried to recoup their money. However, property values often had fallen by then and the real estate wasn't worth anything even close to the amount originally loaned on it. Nevertheless, in order to avoid showing a loss, many of these S&Ls kept trying to recoup impossible dollars. It was sort of like the owner who refuses to admit his or her house has gone down in value and instead keeps trying to get yesterday's prices.

When the RTC takes over the property, however, it sets a list price based on "current appraisals, market surveys, and the recommendation of real estate experts" (*Real Estate Asset Inventory Book*, RTC, June 1990). The new appraisal is not based on what the old S&L had in the property but instead on current values. Thus, when you attempt to buy a property from the RTC, you have a much better chance of getting a realistic value, at least one closer to today's market than yesterday's. The result can be a real bargain.

In short the advantage to you of considering an RTC property is a lower price (and sometimes better terms). It may not always be possible to obtain such a lower price, for reasons we'll discuss next, but when you can, it's well worth your time. This is particularly true since the RTC has properties in virtually every state.

Getting a Bargain Price from the RTC

The RTC does not give away any property. Its goal is to get as much money out of foreclosed property as it can in order to recoup some of the losses of the failed S&Ls. As a result, it is not supposed to sell properties for substantially less than their market value. The FIREE Act of 1989, which helped establish the RTC, in fact, prohibits the organization from selling properties at less than 95 percent of market value in states designated as "distressed areas." (This includes states where the real estate market is severely depressed.)

In states not designated as distressed areas (most of the country including California falls into this category), the RTC has a much freer hand. In these nondistressed states the RTC will often sell its property to the highest bidder. In California, for example, which has relatively few RTC properties, bids have been accepted which were significantly lower than the list price.

Condition of RTC Properties

The RTC does not usually make an effort to improve the condition of its properties. Frequently it will, however, take steps to prevent any further deterioration, such as boarding up the property or putting a fence around it.

As a result, depending on degree of vandalism, if any, the properties can be in anywhere from great to terrible shape. Typically the best bargains come about in properties which have had some vandalism, making them look quite unappealing, but which have not had more than cosmetically repairable damage (broken windows, paint, carpeting, etc.).

It's important to understand that the RTC does not give any warranty regarding the condition of properties it sells. Quite the contrary, in fact, it disclaims any responsibility. Here is a paragraph from an RTC publication:

> The RTC, now and forever, makes no guarantee, warranty, or representation, expressed or implied, as to the location, quality, kind,

character, size, description, or fitness for any use or purpose of any property listed and or described. The RTC does not guarantee that the information contained herein regarding zoning and development opportunities are necessarily accurate or will remain unchanged. All properties are sold in "AS IS" condition. [Capital letters are from the RTC.]

It has been estimated that a sizeable portion of the RTC properties are in such bad condition as to be unsalable. I strongly advise you to carefully examine the property yourself. Getting a bargain price is no bargain if you have to bulldoze the house and start over.

Types of RTC Property

While the RTC owns a great many properties, a very large percentage of them are not residences. These fit into the realm of commercial real estate with a few in the area of land. Those that are residences fit into a variety of distinct areas which include:

Single-family

Multifamily

Condos

Duplexes

Mobile homes

Other residential

As an investor, you can obtain information and make offers on any RTC property. However, as suggested earlier, at least initially you may want to restrict your interests to single-family residential.

Locating Properties

In order to buy an RTC property, you have to know about its existence. The RTC makes this quite simple with easy accessibility from a variety of sources. On the other hand, in order to actually see a property and make an offer, you have to contact a local broker with whom the RTC has a contract. Thus you must, in essence, deal with both the national and the local arm of the corporation. It's not difficult, but it can be complicated.

Trap

Be wary of fly-by-night outfits that purport to sell you "inside" information on buying from the RTC. All the information is readily available direct from the corporation, as indicated below.

RTC Publications and Sources of Information

The RTC publishes a number of books which list properties for sale. As of this writing the books include:

A—Single-Family Residences excluding Texas

B—Single-Family Residences in Texas

C—Multifamily (apartment buildings)

D—Condos

E—Residential Lots

F—Duplexes

G—Mobile Homes

H—Other Residential Properties

These publications consist of page after page of listings that include the following (see also Figure 7-1):

Address

Square footage (for improved properties)

Construction (frame, stucco, etc.)

Bedrooms and baths

Condition (fair, good, excellent)

List price

Asset number

Local broker to contact directly

To order any of the listing books, all you need do is to call 1-800-431-0600. An operator will take your request over the phone and, if you give a major credit card, will promptly send the publication to you. As of this writing the publications cost $15 apiece.

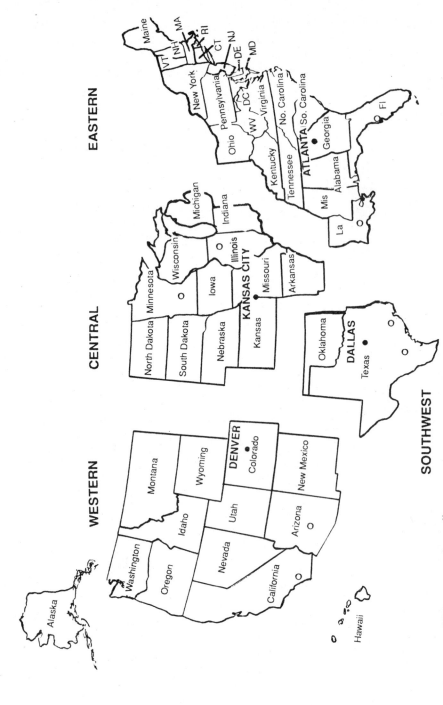

Figure 7-1 RTC regions and site offices.

**Other Methods of Getting RTC
Information**

In addition to the books, the RTC also provides inventory information in the following electronic forms:

CD ROM. The compact disk contains the entire RTC real estate inventory and has sorting capability which allows the user to view targeted assets based on any number of investment criteria. Similar to other compact disks, the user must have specialized equipment, including a computer, to read and sort the data.

On-line access. The RTC also provides on-line data via computer modem. It allows you to produce a hard copy on your own printer and to download the data to a PC file.

Floppy disk. The entire RTC real estate inventory data bank is available on floppy disks. You need to have compatible computer hardware and software to use this format.

Magnetic tape. The format is EBDIC (nine track) and requires sophisticated computer hardware and software.

You can also request information about properties located in a specific city by phone. There is a small charge for this service, but the RTC operator will look up any properties in a category and location that you specify. For information on any of the items listed above call 1-800-431-0600.

Making an Offer

Let's say you've already done your homework. You've called the RTC and found three single-family homes relatively close to you. You have their addresses and the number of the contact broker. What do you do now and what can you expect will happen?

When you call the contact broker, you will most likely discover that he or she is a state licensed real estate broker with an office in an area near the property. In other words, you're dealing with an agent. The agent will have a contract with the RTC to find a buyer for their house. For this the RTC is paying the agent a commission. The broker can arrange for you to get into the property. He or she can also help you with the offer.

The Offer

The offer to purchase is usually made on a standard real estate purchase agreement commonly in use in your state. You make a deposit and submit your offer to the RTC (or to the financial institution if the property happens to be part of a conservatorship, as explained at the beginning of this chapter). If your offer is accepted, the broker will notify you and you have a set time in which to secure financing.

Financing

It's important to understand that the RTC does not want to handle financing for you. Rather, it wants cash for the sale so it can use the money in the S&L bail out. If there are lenders who will loan on the property, you'll have to get financing from them. This part gets a little bit tricky.

On well-located properties, the down payment that lenders require of investors has been typically 20 percent. Most lenders would be willing to loan 80 percent of the balance. Recently, however, with the cold market, some lenders are demanding 25 or even 30 percent down. This is certainly negotiable, of course, and by the time you read this, 20 percent down (or less) may be standard again.

The tricky part is that the RTC will often require that you duplicate your efforts in securing a loan with the lender. In other words, in addition to filling out a loan application (on which you must list all your income, expenses, assets, and liabilities), you must also fill out a similar application with the RTC, even though they're not lending you any money. The same holds true for verifications of deposit and employment and all the other items required as part of a mortgage application. Again, it's not terribly complicated or difficult, but it is tiring and reeks of bureaucratic red tape. Presumably the RTC wants to know who they are selling to in order to ensure that you are a qualified buyer and won't lose the property so that, eventually, they have to take it back again.

Distressed Property

Much of the RTC property can be termed "distressed." That means that either the location is so bad that no one wants it or the property itself is severely damaged. The trouble with distressed property is that no lender may be willing to lend on it. In other words, to buy, you'd have to come up with cash.

Obviously, however, no investor would put cash into property that even a lender wouldn't consider. Thus in order to find a buyer, the RTC may arrange the loan itself. Depending on how distressed the property is, the RTC may make loans of up to 95 percent of the value (only 5 percent down). Keep in mind, of course, that we're not talking about homes in the middle of Beverly Hills. These are almost certainly marginal properties and you want to be sure you've done your homework on them before making any kind of offer.

Closing

The RTC will give clear title, but if you want title insurance (always a good idea), you will probably have to pay for it. In addition because the RTC makes no warranty whatsoever regarding the property, it's a good idea to pay for inspections (including a structural and termite inspection) to be sure that it's not going to fall down 2 hours after you sign the papers.

Special Properties

Some of the properties that the RTC has are designated either "distressed" or "affordable." The distressed properties are not usually listed as such and you will have to do some investigation to find them. We just discussed these in terms of financing. The affordable properties (often also the distressed ones) are indicated as such and may allow special financing and purchase prices to first-time buyers or those who intend to live in the properties. Check with the broker handling individual cases.

For Further Information

The RTC has so many houses and is handling so many failed S&Ls that it's hopeless trying to get additional information (other than inventory lists) from any central location. Rather, the RTC has broken up the country into four major regions, each with its own director. Following is a list, as of this writing, of the directors, the region address, and phone number:

Eastern Region
William M. Dudley, Director
RTC
Marquis 1, Suite 1100
245 Peachtree Center Ave., NE
Atlanta, GA 30303
1-800-234-3342
(404) 522-1145

Central Region
Michael J. Martinelli, Director
RTC
Board of Trade Building II
4900 Main St.
Kansas City, MO 64112
1-800-365-3342
(816) 531-2212

Southwest Region
Carmen J. Sullivan, Director
RTC
1910 Pacific Ave., Suite 1600
Dallas, TX 75201
(214) 953-2300

Western Region
Anthony Scalzi, Director
RTC
1515 Arapahoe St., Tower 3,
  Suite 800
Denver, CO 80202
(303) 556-6500

In addition there are contacts in many S&Ls or other lending institutions who can give you information on specific properties as well as help to arrange for financing. RTC books contain a list of these institutions. In each case ask to speak to the REO marketing department. *Note*: This list is subject to change and to error on the part of the RTC, which compiles it.

8

Buying Bank-Owned Real Estate (REOs)

REO stands for real estate owned. If you're a financial officer in a lending institution, those are the three letters you never want to hear.

Lending institutions and in particular S&Ls are in business primarily to make loans and collect interest. They need to collect that interest in order to pay out interest on deposits and, hence, to remain solvent. As a result, the most important officer in a lending institution is the one who makes loans, good loans. (A good loan is one which the borrower repays on time.) A lending officer who makes good loans can be highly rewarded.

The problem is that usually there is far more money to lend out than there are qualified borrowers for it. As a result, lending officers are caught between a rock and a hard place. If they produce the volume their employer wants, they are bound to get some bad loans. If they go only for good loans, they can't keep up the volume. As a result, almost all lending institutions have problem loans. And the turnover rate for lending officers tends to be high.

Since most of the money loaned by S&Ls goes to real estate, they tend to have a significant amount of problem mortgages. (While this is generally true, there are some exceptionally well run S&Ls who have almost no problem loans.)

In the last chapter we talked about how the RTC stepped in and took over S&Ls that had so many bad loans that they were declared insolvent by the government. However, there are also many thousands of S&Ls across the country that while maintaining sufficient reserves to be considered solvent, still have problem mortgages. These are the ones we are going to deal with in this chapter—the solvent S&Ls with problems.

Understanding the S&L's Perspective

When a mortgage is performing, that is, the borrower is repaying on time, that mortgage is considered an asset of the S&L. However, once the borrower stops repaying, after a period of time (usually 90 to 180 days), the S&L is required to move that mortgage from the performing category to the nonperforming list. S&Ls are not allowed to consider nonperforming mortgages for their full value as an asset. Rather, a percentage is considered a liability.

This affects the bottom line of the S&L's balance sheet. In these days of increased capital requirements and much closer scrutiny by the government, an S&L has to be very careful about how many properties it allows to slip into the nonperforming category.

Once a property is nonperforming for a period of time and the borrower appears unable to correct the deficiencies, the lender will begin foreclosure. (Contrary to popular belief, most lenders do not start foreclosure when the first payment is late. Typically they will wait 3 to 6 months before even beginning foreclosure proceedings.)

The loan remains nonperforming throughout the foreclosure process. However, once the foreclosure is complete and the lender takes title to the property, the mortgage stops being nonperforming. It, in fact, stops being a mortgage at all. It is erased from the mortgage category and is instead placed on the books as a property valued for the amount of the mortgage. The property becomes an REO.

That property, in theory, is an asset. However, since it produces no interest, it in actuality is a liability. It is the S&L's capital tied up with no interest payments coming in. It doesn't take long for an S&L to get into capital reserve troubles if it has too many REOs. Ten mortgages of $100,000 apiece converted to REOS ties up a million dollars.

It is to the S&L's advantage, therefore, to get rid of that property as soon as possible. It wants to sell it and thus convert the REO back into either cash, which can be loaned out, or a new mortgage, which comes to the same thing.

The point of this discussion is to make clear that *S&Ls don't want REOS in the worst way.* They will do almost anything to get rid of any they have, including making you a sweetheart deal on them. Some of the best deals in a cold market can be obtained by buying S&L REOs.

REOs Today

There are always REOs on the market. As noted earlier, it is an exceptional S&L that doesn't have any at all. Most are always processing a few. However, when the market turns down in real estate, the number of borrowers who don't pay increases. *Consider*: Let's say that you bought a house at the top of the market for $200,000 and you put 10 percent, or $20,000 down, so you had a $180,000 mortgage. Now the market has fallen so that your house is only worth $160,000. In other words, it's worth $20,000 less than your mortgage.

Would you keep making mortgage payments? Interestingly enough, most people do. They do so either because they are extremely honest or because they want to preserve their good credit or because it's easier to do so than to figure a way out of the problem—so they keep on paying.

However, if they happen to get ill or lose their job (job loss is the largest single reason for foreclosure in this country today) or something else untoward happens, things change. Now, they stop making those payments on a house worth less than its mortgage. They just let the house go and take their chances with their credit.

Hence, when the market turns down, the number of foreclosures increases dramatically. (Often this increase precedes the downturn. For example, at the depth of the recent S&L crisis the number of foreclosures was actually *decreasing*, most having been processed earlier.)

Even good S&Ls have trouble with increased numbers of REOs in down times. And that's where you come in. You're going to help out those good S&Ls. You're going to take over some of their problem property.

The Great REO Secret

There is one stumbling block, however. Almost universally, S&Ls won't admit publicly that they have an REO problem. Most won't admit they even have any REOs. This certainly seems to work against their best interests, at least on the surface. One would think that they would be out there advertising those properties as heavily as possible. Yet, they don't. Do you ever recall seeing a lender advertising under its own name for REO buyers? It normally just doesn't happen. (Most of the public isn't even familiar with the term "REO.")

The reasoning of the S&Ls is threefold. First, an S&L doesn't want to alert federal watchdogs that it has an REO problem. With the feds taking over hundreds of insolvent S&Ls, they really don't have many people left to watch out for the marginal ones. Keeping up a good face can mean the difference between remaining in business or being taken over by the RTC.

Second, depositors these days are very uncomfortable about where they place their money. We've all heard too many stories of lending institutions going belly up. Yes, we know every account is guaranteed for $100,000. But, how many of us want to put that guarantee to the test? We might bolt if we thought the S&L was shaky.

In addition there are holders of amounts larger than $100,000 who frequently move funds from lender to lender trying to tie up the highest interest rates. These large depositors are not technically insured and will pull their funds from a lending institution at the slightest whiff of trouble. Hence, S&Ls are very careful not to admit they have many REOs if for no other reason than to protect their own image.

Finally, there is the matter of the real estate market. If it got widely known that S&Ls had an overhang of homes ready to dump on the market, it would further depress prices. This would backfire for the S&Ls since it would result in their receiving less money for the properties they are trying to sell.

Therefore, the S&Ls are close-mouthed about their REOs because:

1. They don't want to alert federal watchdogs.

2. They don't want to scare away depositors.

3. They don't want to hurt the fragile real estate market.

Finding Out About REOs

All of the above reasons present a problem for you, who want to get an especially good deal in a cold market. How do you find out about REOs when the lenders keep mum about them? Well, the truth is that while lenders keep quiet about REOs as far as the general public is concerned, they can be open about them to investors. Investors, after all, are who they sell most of the REOS to. That includes you.

What you have to do to find REOs is both complex and simple. It's complex because you have to do it over and again for each lender. It's simple because the process is quite easy. Basically you need to let a lender know that you are a sophisticated investor. You need to let the lender know that you understand what an REO is and that you'd like to bid on one. Once the lender understands that you're special and not part of the general buying public, they will open up, in a limited way.

For example, I recently called up the main offices of a large lender in the San Francisco bay area. I asked to talk to the officer in charge of the REO department. For a few minutes the operator seem confused. They had a loan department, an escrow department, an operations officer. She didn't have an REO department listed. I asked to talk to the operations officer. (The operations officer handles day-to-day operations of the lending institution.) I explained to her that I was an investor and wanted to speak to someone in the REO department. I was given a number to call.

When I called the number I explained I was an investor interested in purchasing an REO. Could I get a list of REOs available from the lending institution? No, I was told. No such list existed. (Hah! The S&L didn't have a list of its own REOs? Come on, now.)

I understood that I was just a voice on the other end of the line. I was someone unknown to the REO officer who wasn't about to release information considered delicate. So I tried a different ploy. I said I was looking for REOs in a particular area. I gave the community, a rather small district of the city. Did the S&L have any REOs in that area? There was a pause, then the officer was saying that yes, there were three. If I was interested in them I could come down and fill out an identity form and they would then give me the addresses so I could go out and look them over.

Success! As I said, it really isn't hard. But you have to do it for each lender and it's a little bit different each time.

Working with Agents

Sometimes when you call a lender you will be told that all REOs are listed with local real estate agents. The agents handle the sale for the lender who has no direct sales to the public. Fine. Deal with the agent.

I have successfully bought REOs through agents. If the lender wants to pay a commission to a broker for handling the sale, it's no skin off my knee. Typically a lender will designate a particular broker to handle all its REOs in an area. Usually it is one of the larger and more active offices.

After you find out who the agent is from the lender, just call up the office and ask to speak to "Jackie Jones," who handles the REOs for "XYZ" S&L. Usually there is one agent who does this, although in large offices sometimes all the agents "co-broke," or work on, REO sales.

Talk to the agent. Explain you're an investor looking for a good REO deal. Get to know the agent a bit and allow him or her to get to know you.

Making a Backup offer

Typically you will be told that the agent doesn't have any REOs from the S&L *at the present time.* The reason is quite simple. These are good deals and they sell quickly.

I can recall one REO I bought a few years ago in this manner from an agent. When told there were none available, I asked if any had recently been sold. Yes, I was told. One had, but it was in escrow. "Fine," I said. "Could I see it?" "Certainly." I was given the address and the agent later took me to the property. It was a nice house, run down, but in a good area and at a good price. I said I would like to make a "back up" offer on it. If the current offer fell through, I'd like mine to be considered.

Fine, said the agent, and wrote it up. My reasoning was quite simple. Most active investors, those who own lots of property, are spread thin. As a result, they often have little cash to put down or their income isn't sufficient to cover all their properties. In addition, over the years they have lost one or two properties and the foreclosures show up on their credit reports. They may even be land poor, owning several valuable properties, but unable to get their cash out. These active investors frequently know about REOs and often make offers which are accepted. But also, frequently, these people don't qualify for financing.

This happened to be the case with me. The first buyer was rejected for a mortgage by the lender. My back-up offer, already written up, was submitted. And subsequently, I got the property.

No, it won't happen that way every time. But, it will happen that way often enough to make it worthwhile trying.

Condition of REOs

REOs are often in distressed condition. If you were the borrower and were losing the house, your equity, your credit rating, would you be anxious to keep watering the lawn or to clean up when you left?

Most borrowers who lose their property through foreclosure not only do not clean up, but they actually go out of their way to mess up the property. Their reaction, naturally enough, is anger and since they really can't take it out on anyone personally, they typically take it out on the property.

I have seen REOs where the sinks and toilets were ripped out, where all the windows were broken, where fecal material was rubbed into the carpets, where holes were smashed into the walls and on and on. (I've often speculated that had the former owners spent half as much energy trying to make the payments as they did messing up the house, they might still own the property.)

When you get to the REO, it may still be in the terrible shape in which the lender got it back. Or it may be fixed up. Lenders are no fools (although their lending policies often suggest otherwise). They know that a distressed property will get them a distressed price. On the other hand, if they fix it up even just cosmetically, they stand to get a far better price.

The problem with fixing it up in today's market, however, is that since sales volume is so low, they have to wait months to get a good price even after the property is fixed up. In their desperation to get the REO off the books, it might be worthwhile to sell it immediately "as is" for far less.

Again, that's where you come in. When you find a distressed REO, don't turn your head away in disgust. You're not looking at a disaster; you may be looking at an opportunity.

Calculating Fix-Up and Cleanup

Experienced investors can do this in just a few minutes. But, that's a result of their experience. If you're new to the game, it's going to take you longer. If you find a distressed REO that otherwise fits your needs in terms of location, tenant market, etc. (see earlier chapters), calculate the costs to fix it up.

You may have to call out a painter, plumber, and electrician. (In truth, to be successful, you're going to have to eventually make contact with those who can do this for you or you're going to have to learn how to do it yourself.) You may have to calculate the costs of having someone come in and clean out the mess. You'll have to calculate relandscaping costs and so forth. Here are some of the items you need to consider:

Cleanup (Including washing kitchen appliances such as stove and sink and baths.)

Cleaning or replacing carpeting and pads (Watch out for pet urine in the carpet—often the smell cannot be removed and the carpet must be replaced.)

Plumbing (Including replacing fixtures such as baths, sinks, and toilets.)

Electrical (Putting in new light fixtures and repairing any damage.)

Painting (Inside and out where needed.)

Landscaping (Including new front lawn and garden—you can often get by without fixing up the back yard.)

Fencing (Often this is broken down.)

Roof (Check for leaks.)

Plaster or wall board repair (Fix holes.)

Doors and door handles (Replace or repair.)

Windows and screens (Replace.)

As you can see, the list is fairly long. It can also be fairly costly. It's important that you get as accurate a cost figure as possible. Remember, you'll be paying for it. Also, don't forget to include a figure for your time and effort, especially if you're going to be doing the work yourself.

Trap

Often distressed properties are in distressed neighborhoods. Remember to judge the neighborhood first and foremost. Don't become enraptured with dreams of refurbishing the house until you're convinced that the neighborhood warrants it. If there's a high crime and vandalism rate in the neighborhood, you may find that as quickly as you clean up and fix up, there's someone coming around to tear down and mess up. That's a hopeless situation, one of the worst, and you want to avoid it at all costs.

Making an Offer

Once you've done your homework in determining that the REO is a good prospect in terms of location, rental market, etc., as outlined earlier and you've determined the costs to bring it into rentable shape, you need to determine what you're going to offer the lender.

Keep in mind that everything in real estate especially including an REO is negotiable. The lender may have set a price, but you don't have to pay it. You can make a lower offer or you can ask for favorable terms.

Tip

Good REO property is in high demand by investors. Keep in mind that there may be many offers on the house you are considering. The lender, naturally enough, is going to accept the best.

As a consequence, you need to make your offer as sweet as possible, without hurting. I can recall one REO investor who beat me out on a house a few years back by offering nearly $10,000 more than me. The lender, who I knew fairly well, asked me if I wanted to raise my offer. I reexamined my figures and declined. I couldn't see a profit for me at the higher costs. So the lender gave the property to the other bidder.

As it turned out, she later admitted that she had overpaid and lost money on the deal. Remember, getting the property is only one battle. Winning the war means ultimately making a profit. If there's no profit, you're just spinning your wheels.

The Cash Offer

With a distressed property there are a variety of ways to make an offer. The simplest (for the lender, not you) is to offer all cash. This doesn't mean that you need all cash—you can go out and secure financing on the property. It just means that the lender is going to get all cash.

Typically how you arrive at a price for a cash deal is to calculate what the property is going to be worth when it's fixed up, given the current market conditions. Then work backward subtracting your realistic costs of fixing it up. (Don't forget to deduct interest payments during the fix up period.)

The trouble with an all-cash offer is twofold. From the lender's perspective, it means selling for what probably amounts to a substantial loss. From your perspective, it means going out and finding a separate, new lender who is willing to loan you money on a distressed property—not something easy to find in today's cold market. There may be an easier way.

Offering Terms

A better way that I have used is to offer the lender terms. Offer full market price for the property. In other words, you determine what the house would be worth given the current conditions, but after it's fully fixed up. You offer that price. However, you then request something like the following:

1. The lender makes you a 90 percent loan on that full purchase price at a favorable interest rate for a term of at least 5 years (based on a 30-year amortization). (This allows you time to fix-up, rent, and hold until the market turns. It also guarantees the lender that it will be out of the property for good after a set amount of time.)

2. The lender gives you a fix-up allowance equal to your costs of refurbishing the property, all of which is *to come out of the new loan*. This sim-

ply means that the lender will give you cash back out of the new mortgage (typically made in payments as the work is completed) to fix up
the property.

3. The lender pays normal closing costs.

The above terms will appeal to a lender for several reasons. The first
is the price. It can show the property was sold at full market price and
that it now has a, presumably, performing mortgage on it—an *asset*. Second, the lender doesn't have to go in and spend time and money fixing
up the property itself, something which many lenders are ill-prepared to
do. Third, you are guaranteeing to fix up the property so that in the
event you don't make your payments and the lender has to re-foreclose,
it should be getting the property back in far better shape.

The above is usually an appealing offer. Most lenders will take it, unless there is someone who's got a sharper pencil than you and offered
more or asked for a lesser allowance. (Remember, don't lower your offer
or terms just to compete—you could turn a profitable deal into a loser.)

Traps in REOs

It has been estimated that something approaching half of all REOs (including RTC properties) are distressed and that many of these are hopeless. If you're looking at distressed properties, it's important to determine which have possibilities and which are hopeless. The last thing you
want to do is to relieve a lender of a hopeless problem and make it yours.

The important thing to remember is that the REO is most often sold
as is. The lender and/or seller makes no commitment to you of any
kind. This can result in some bizarre and horrifying problems.

Unexpected Costs

For example, one investor I know, Jason, bought an REO with a "cracked
slab." In his area of the country, houses were typically built on slabs of
concrete reinforced with steel instead of the more common peripheral
foundation and raised wood floor. Jason's house seemed all right to look
at. However, it was on a slight hill and one side near the kitchen and din-
ing room sank slightly where the slab was cracked.

Jason evaluated it carefully. He even called in a contractor to examine
it. The conclusion was that the ground under the slab at the kitchen had
moved outward slightly causing the slab to fall. At the worst it was offset
about three inches. The contractor said that to fix it completely, he'd

have to rip down half the house and rebuild. But cosmetically, he figured he could just pour a new layer over the slab, lift up the walls, and the house would be ready to go.

A simple thing to correct, Jason thought. He made an offer on the REO based on the cosmetic change and was successful. A short time later, the house was his.

However, problems appeared as soon as he started refurbishing. It turned out that when the contractor began cutting out pieces of the old slab in order to blend in the new layer of concrete, he discovered that the reinforcing steel was missing. The original builder some 30 years earlier had failed to put it in.

Without steel, the cracked slab was free to move wherever it wanted. Putting a new layer of concrete on the top wouldn't help at all. The new layer would quickly crack, and perhaps sink, as the concrete continued to shift.

In addition the local building department showed up to ask why the contractor was working without a permit. (A neighbor had seen the work and complained.) The contractor immediately stopped work and applied for a permit, which was denied. The building department said that, given the lack of reinforcing steel, the only way it would allow work to proceed was to tear out the old cement (and half the house) and put in new cement and new steel.

This story does not have a happy ending. Jason complained to the lender and eventually threatened a lawsuit. The lender finally agreed to take back the property without reporting a default to Jason's credit, although it admitted no blame seeing as Jason had signed an as is clause. But Jason's original down payment and money spent refurbishing were lost.

Existing Tenants Who Won't Leave

Another problem in an REO happened to Phyllis. She bought a property which, fortunately, had no cracked slab. It did, however, have a tenant in it. The tenant was there when she examined the property and claimed that he was paying rent to the lender. Fine, Janet thought. Having a tenant already in place will save me some time and money. She went ahead with the purchase buying the property as is.

Once the deal went through, she went back and introduced herself as the new owner. She told the tenant that he should now pay the rent to her and she showed him the title papers. He slammed the door in her face, wouldn't let her in, and refused to talk to her.

As it turned out, he had been the tenant of the original owner who had rented out the property instead of living in it personally. When the property went into foreclosure, the tenant remained, not paying rent. He hadn't paid rent for the past 5 months and wasn't about to start now.

Janet tried to reason with him, but to no avail. Eventually she had to secure the services of a real estate attorney who, for several thousand dollars and after a period of 9 weeks, finally had the man evicted. During that time, of course, Janet couldn't fix up the property, yet she had to make mortgage payments, pay taxes, and insurance.

The moral here is beware of any REO that has anyone living in it. It could be a former tenant or a former owner. Regardless, *never* take possession and close the deal until the property is vacant. Otherwise, you could be tying yourself into a real headache. (Janet was lucky in a sense. If the tenant had declared bankruptcy or was a pregnant woman or was seriously ill, depending on the state, he or she might be allowed to stay in the place indefinitely.)

REOs can be a great opportunity, if you take the time to find out about them and then use your calculator carefully.

9
Buying at Auction

Whenever the price of real estate falls, auctions appear. One has to wonder, where do all the auctioneers go when the market is up? In a strong real estate market there are virtually no auctioneers. But, just let the market go down and they seem to come out of the woodwork.

If you're in an area of the country where the real estate market is depressed, you surely have seen auctions advertised. I'm sure you have also wondered if they are a good deal. Perhaps you've gone to one or two and not bid and still wondered, can I get a really good buy at a real estate auction?

In this chapter we'll look at real estate auctions, the benefits they offer, and the pitfalls to avoid. We'll take a close look at their appeal and their reality.

What Are Auctions?

Auctions as a means of selling a commodity are not new. They're ancient. They are a tried and true method of selling that date back to the bazaars of ancient Mesopotamia. In an auction, owners of commodities consign their wares to an auctioneer. The auctioneer, a person skilled in dealing with crowds of buyers, has told the owners that he can sell their merchandise for them and get a good price for it. They trust him. They put their faith in his hands.

Auctions involving real estate are a relatively new phenomenon and occur only occasionally. Therefore, before looking at them directly, it is instructive to consider auctions in general. We'll do this by looking at an area where auctions have been going on for decades and occur on a regular weekly, even daily basis—rare coin auctions.

Rare coin auctions are constantly being held by dealers across the country. The dealers advertise the auctions in splashy full-color brochures, in trade papers and in magazines, and even on elaborate computer link-ups with other dealers.

Auctions Pros and Cons

What they advertise are availability and bargains. A rare coin, like a rare painting, often has many people clamoring for it. The auctions allow the potential buyers to bid one against the other and thus achieve the highest price for the seller. Therefore for the seller, liquidity and the possibility of a high price are the big incentives.

But there is a drawback to the seller. What if only one person bids and that is a low-ball bid? The rare coin could be sold for a fraction of its true value. To avoid this possibility, most sales are "reserve" sales. This means that there is a minimum price below which the seller will refuse to sell, the reserve. (Often the reserve in rare coin auctions is not announced.)

In reality virtually all auctions are reserve sales. Few sellers are willing to take a chance that because of poor weather or competition from other sales or just freak occurrence there will be only a few low bids. Those who do sell without reserve usually live to regret it.

One rare coin dealer whom I know put up a coin conservatively worth $50,000 a few years ago, without reserve. It was a bold thing to do and he did it, ostensibly, to draw more people to the auction. He regretted it. The winning bid was $10,000. The coin was sold, he got $10,000 and lost $40,000. You can be sure he'll never enter a sale without a reserve again.

Of course, from the buyer's perspective, the auction holds out the promise of a bargain. The thought is always present in the buyer's mind that he or she might get a steal. What if you put in a low bid and, for some strange reason, no one else bids? You can get a rare coin for half its real value. You could instantly take it out and resell it at a huge profit.

Hence buyers are more likely to attend auctions that have no reserve or auctions where the reserve is not announced and buyers are unaware of its existence. It is the matter of the reserve that is the biggest attraction as well as the biggest stumbling block in the world of auctions.

Real Estate Auctions

Real estate auctions are both similar to and different from rarity auctions. For one thing, there's the merchandise. In a rare coin sale (or sale of a painting or other artwork), the owner usually owns the item free and clear. Not so in real estate. Here, the item is almost universally mortgaged. The bank owns most of it. So what is the owner selling? He or she is selling equity, his or her equity or interest in the property. (We'll talk about bank auctions shortly.)

This has important consequences for the auction. While in a rare coin auction, the price has at least the potential of falling virtually to zero, at a real estate auction (nonbank) the price can fall only as low as the seller's equity. Below that point he or she doesn't own the property.

Tip

Most real estate auctions are of two varieties. In the one there are builders trying to get rid of unsold new homes. In the other you have a lender trying to dump foreclosed property, often new homes taken back from a builder who was unable to sell them.

Recently there have been occasional auctions where an auctioneer puts together a group of individual sellers, each selling his or her own house. Usually the houses are in close proximity to one another and the prices are relatively close as well. This is a much more uncommon kind of auction but one which I would make it a point of attending, since it might offer the best opportunity for getting a true bargain.

Let's consider a typical builder's auction. A builder or developer has put up a "spec" tract of homes. While some have sold, ten houses remain and, given the current real estate climate, cannot be sold. So she decides to hold an auction to get rid of them. The houses have been priced at $200,000 apiece. The builder owes the bank $150,000 apiece. In other words her equity is $50,000 a house.

The builder hires an auctioneer. The auctioneer places ads in the local papers, inserts 30-second spots on the local radio station, and pastes billboards at all the grocery and service stores in the area. Flyers are even distributed to local home owners and special announcements are sent to all the local real estate offices and anyone identified as a potential buyer or investor. All of these announce the day, place, and time of the auction, the property to be auctioned, and what wonderful bargains are going to be available.

When the auction day arrives and the first house is put up for sale, the auctioneer asks for bids starting at $175,000 which he says is $25,000 less than the previous asking price for the houses. There are no bids.

The auctioneer drops his price. "Will anyone start out at $165,000. Come on folks, this is a $35,000 bargain!" Again there are no bids.

The auctioneer looks exasperated and says, "Well folks, let's go one last time. Will anyone bid $150,000. That's 25 percent off the 'market value.' Surely someone out there wants to pocket the $50,000 difference?" Again no bids. So the auctioneer says, "You know what. Maybe no one wants this house. So let's try the next one."

On and on it goes with the auctioneer eventually getting some bids and probably selling some houses, all above the $150,000 level below which the builder can't go. (For purposes of this example we've overlooked the auctioneer's commission, which comes out of the sales price.)

Usually the reserve, in this case $150,000, is announced, though through clever manipulation the auctioneer never lets the price dip below $150,000 without mentioning the reserve.

Absolute Auctions

Not all auctions are like the one described above. Sometimes, particularly in severely depressed real estate markets, "absolute" auctions really are held. These are auctions in which there is no reserve. Typically the seller is a lender who holds clear title to the property after taking it back in foreclosure.

Here, because there is no mortgage holder (the seller being the former mortgage holder) the sale moves forward at whatever price is obtained. Here the buyer can truly obtain a very low-priced property.

The problem, of course, is that absolute auctions are almost always held only when the market is absolutely bad. They have been held in parts of New England and in Texas. Typically they involve property that has been vandalized in areas where no one wants to live. Often the property has already dropped down close to zero value, so that the seller really doesn't have a whole lot to lose by offering an absolute sale.

Thus you, the buyer, typically will come up against two kinds of auctions—the reserve auction, which usually involves desirable properties, and the absolute auction, which involves properties that you may not really want.

Trap

Beware of *phony* absolute auctions. Auctioneers are well aware that 3 times as many buyers show up at an absolute auction as at a reserve auction. Consequently, some may advertise valuable property as an absolute sale when it really isn't.

At these auctions if the bidding is too low (below the hidden reserve), there always seem to be one or two bidders in the audience who bid the prices higher. Because of these one or two, no properties are sold at a really low price.

Of course, these "bidders" in the audience in actuality may be "shills" (in the parlance of the gambling trade). They may be there to stimulate bidding but also to be sure that no properties are sold at a really low level.

Many states have created laws that prohibit the seller or his agents from bidding on property at an absolute auction, the intent being to prevent shills from forcing the price up. In actual practice, however, it's very hard to prove that someone is a shill. The person could be a relative or friend of the seller who, ostensibly, really is interested in buying. So what if a month after the auction the deal falls through and no sale is made? Who's to know?

In my experience when I see one or two people at a so-called absolute auction preventing the properties from being sold at a low price, I leave. I just have to assume that whether or not it's against the law, some shenanigans are taking place.

Can You Get a Good Deal?

Having gone to more than a few auctions in my time, my own experience is that, yes, you can get a deal that's better than the market price. But no, it's usually no better than you could have gotten had you gone directly to the seller yourself and made a low-ball offer.

Tip

Beware of the all hoopla that's often presented at an auction. Sometimes they will be held in a beautiful white tent with balloons and streamers. There may be free food and wine tasting. (It should go without saying you should never drink intoxicating beverages while you're conducting real estate or any other kind of business.) The auctioneer and his or her associates may be dressed in tuxedoes. The whole thing may have an up-scale "event" beat to it.

Don't be fooled. The atmosphere is carefully orchestrated to create a "group mentality" calculated to make you loosen your wallet and to think that you're getting a great deal, when you're not. It still all comes back to dollars and common sense. The auctioneers can put a washed face on it, but it's still a hard sell and you'd be wise to always keep one hand on your wallet.

Terms and Conditions of an Auction

Auctions usually have in common the terms and conditions they impose. While these will differ between auctioneers and states, there are several similarities which can be noted.

Deposit

Auctioneers want as many people to attend their auctions as possible, but they want those people to be qualified. Lookers who walk in off the street to sample the food and drink are not wanted. Therefore the auctioneers will often insist that everyone who attends either submit to a credit check before hand or come with a certified check or cash for a minimum amount of money, often around $2500. These are your tickets into the auction and may actually be collected. The big question that most people ask is, is it refundable?

The answer is yes—and no. At an auction, you're not required to bid. If you put up a deposit and don't bid on a property, you should get it back. However, I have seen auctions where the auctioneers suggest that the prices are going to be so phenomenally low that only those who put up a *nonrefundable* deposit will be allowed into the bidding. In other words, your deposit will be credited toward any purchases you make, but if you fail to make any purchases, you lose it.

It's not clear to me that such a nonrefundable deposit involving real estate is legal in most states. Nevertheless, legal or not, possession is nine-tenths of the law and if the auctioneer has your $2500 deposit, it could cost a lot more than that to try to get it back in court.

My suggestion is that unless you have some inside knowledge that convinces you that the auction really will be a barn burner, you should stay away. Simply don't attend any auction where the deposit is nonrefundable. If possible, never even give the auction company your check until you've made a purchase. (Your good credit should suffice.) If there's any suggestion about the refundability of the deposit, don't put it up. It could be like tossing money down a bottomless hole.

On the other hand, what if you are the successful bidder? In that case your deposit is considered earnest money, an actual deposit on the property. If you don't follow through with the purchase, the auction company would be reasonably entitled to keep it.

But what if you don't qualify or you lose your job between the time you make the winning bid and when you need to come up with the balance? This gets tricky. A lot depends on how the purchase contract that you sign is worded. In a good contract, you will get your money back if you are prevented by outside forces (such as not qualifying for a mortgage) from completing the deal. In a bad contract you lose the money regardless. Read the contract carefully. It probably is binding.

Trap

You may agree to agree to contract terms before you actually do the bidding. When you put up your deposit (refundable if you don't bid or aren't successful), the contract you sign may specify under what conditions, if any, the deposit is refundable if you are successful. Read everything you sign and be sure you understand it.

Qualifying for a Mortgage

Unlike rare coins, no one expects you come up with cash when you bid on a property. It is assumed you'll get a mortgage. Often the auctioneer will help you get it. Sometimes, however, what the auctioneer can arrange might not have as favorable terms as you might be able to handle yourself.

My suggestion is that you get "prequalifed." Many lenders, especially large banks, S&Ls, and mortgage bankers, are able to do this. It usually just means introducing yourself and providing the credit and income information that is normally given when you apply for a mortgage. Only this time, you provide it before you get the mortgage.

The lender looks you over, financially, and then tells you how big a mortgage you can have, assuming the property qualifies. Be sure that this prequalification is in writing and that it involves a "commitment to lend." This commitment is all important because it means that when you land the property, you just call up the lender, an appraisal is made, and if the house qualifies, the money is available.

Terms and Conditions

There are a number of terms and conditions you want to watch out for before you sign anything at an auction.

Title. Be sure that you are to be given clear title and that it is backed up by a policy of title insurance. Buying a property with a "clouded" title or one on which someone else has a claim is one can of worms you want to avoid.

Escrow. Be sure that there are provisions made for an adequate escrow. An escrow is an independent third party, typically a state licensed escrow company, that holds your money until the title is transferred. You may end up putting tens of thousands of dollars down and you don't want to trust this money to the auctioneer or the seller. If they disappear with it, you could have to stand the loss.

Time Constraints.   Understand the time constraints. Typically you will only have a couple of weeks to get a mortgage and come up with the down payment. In my experience, the auctioneers and the sellers are often willing to extend the time as necessary. After all, they want to make a sale, too. But they don't have to.

Trap

Perhaps the worst problem with buying at an auction is that unless you're very knowledgeable about real estate, you're at the mercy of the auctioneer. You may need the help of a competent real estate attorney, but you may not have one around when you are required to sign papers that commit you to making a deal or coming up with money.

My suggestion is that unless you're very knowledgeable, stay away from the auctions. *Or,* hire an attorney or someone whose knowledge and experience you trust to accompany you and advise you on everything to sign and do. *Don't rely on the advice of the seller or the auctioneer.* They aren't in your corner.

Real estate auctions are two-sided. On the one hand they offer opportunity. On the other, they can be dangerous.

10
How to Shop for Government Repos

We've talked about RTC properties and the REOs of financial institutions in the previous two chapters. Now, let's consider opportunities offered by a different kind of foreclosed property—one owned by the Federal Housing Administration (FHA).

The FHA was born in the late 1930s as an answer to the great depression. People back then had trouble getting mortgages on property because banks were not willing to make long-term loans. The FHA, on the other hand, was willing to make a then unheard of loan for a term of 10 years with only about 5 percent down. In truth, the FHA revolutionized American housing. In many ways it was to housing after the great depression what the Marshall Plan was to economic recovery in Europe after the Second World War.

Unfortunately, over time things changed. During the Reagan years, FHA large projects loans were frequently made to friends of those in government regardless of the economic soundness of the project or the ability of the borrower to repay. FHA loans to individuals were made without carefully scrutinizing loan documents to see whether the borrowers could repay or whether appraisals on the properties were truly a reflection of market price.

As a result the number of FHA repos (repossessions or foreclosed properties) began to climb steadily in the early 1980s. In the mid-1980s the numbers declined momentarily as a mini-real estate boom hit much of the country. But, by the end of the last decade the numbers of foreclosed properties were skyrocketing once again.

Within the past few years FHA lending policies have tightened dramatically, which will help reduce the number of repos in the future. But for now, there are literally ten of thousands of them all across the country. Some of these may be an opportunity for you.

Problems with FHA Repos

Before getting your hopes up, keep in mind that perhaps as many as a third of the FHA repos currently in the government's inventory are hopeless properties. Either they are so badly located or they are so distressed or the market in their areas is so bad that they literally can't be sold. That means that they don't meet current FHA lending standards and no other lender will loan on them either.

If you happen to have a lot of cash and want some real bargains, you might check with the local FHA office in your area. The government may eventually have to dispose of these properties for a few cents on the dollar. (You had also better be fabulous at refurbishing and renting property in blighted areas, if you get one or more of these.)

Refurbished FHA Repos

Of the remaining repos which are not hopeless, the FHA has two disposal programs. In the first, it comes in and completely rehabilitates the house. It fixes anything that's broken, puts in new carpeting, paints, and so on. When the crews are done, you'd swear the place was new.

It then puts the property on the market. Typically the FHA will allow a 5 percent commission to brokers who bring in buyers, but it won't list with any one broker. Rather, in order to buy, you (either directly or through a broker) work with the FHA.

For these houses, the FHA gets a true appraisal of the market and then, typically, asks a bit more. It figures, apparently, that since the house is already fixed up, often better than its neighbors, it should be entitled to top dollar.

In addition, the FHA finances the purchase. If you intend to live in the property, you may only have to come up with 5 percent down. Of course, you'll have to have excellent credit and show a strong ability to repay (have a high enough income).

These terms tend to work against investors. Most investors, perhaps including you, really don't intend to live in the property. Rather, you anticipate buying and then renting.

If that's the case, the FHA would rather not finance the sale. It would prefer that you come in with cash (at its relatively high price), getting the money from another lender. In some areas it will allow you to get an FHA mortgage on the property, but typically the minimum down payment required will be 15 percent (instead of a much lower 5 for buyers who intend to live in the property).

As a result, the refurbished FHA properties are not usually considered good buys from an investment standpoint. If you're a first-time home buyer looking for a place to live, they could be an excellent choice. If you're an investor, however, you probably could do better elsewhere.

As Is FHAs

In addition to the refurbished homes, the FHA also offers a large number of homes sold as is. These include the hopeless properties noted above as well as some not so hopeless. If you're a discriminating investor, this could be your best government repo opportunity.

The list of FHA repos, if any, offered on an as is basis in your area is available from the FHA. It also is frequently available from most brokers until the deadline for filing a offer (the FHA accepts offers on these properties typically right up to a certain date they set). It is many times published in a paper of local circulation. It's not hard to find out about FHA repos.

Once you get hold of the list, however, the real work begins. Now, you have to trudge out to each property and examine it. Typically the properties are locked, so you won't be able to get in. But, you will be able to scout out the general area, nearby neighborhood, overall condition of the property, and the tenant market. In short, you should be able to make a pretty good estimate if the property is worth fooling with or not. If it is, the FHA will give you a local broker to contact who has the key and you can then get in to inspect the interior.

Making the Offer

If you find a good FHA repo, one that you like, and want to make an offer, my suggestion is that you contact a local broker involved in the program. The brokers are familiar with the procedure in use in your area and can make dealing with the FHA a lot simpler. Besides, the government pays them a commission, not you. The price is the same whether or not you use a broker.

Although the FHA is not supposed to take less than 5 percent below the appraised value on an as is property, you can offer what you want. If the property has been advertised once at market value and there were no offers, the FHA may offer to sell the property to the highest bidder, subject to acceptance of a government review officer.

_____

There have been so many FHA properties placed on the market recently that the organization has had difficulty keeping up. The sheer numbers of its inventory may make the buying process frustratingly slow for you. Just hang in there. Eventually it will all get done.

Knowing what to bid is a bit like playing poker. You have to guess if there are other bidders and what they might offer. You also have to guess how anxious the FHA is to dump this property.

Not long ago I made a bid on an FHA property in southern California. I estimated that its market value was around $150,000. It was, however, in terrible shape and I estimated it would cost about $15,000 to make it rentable.

Since I judged the market to be at bottom at the time in the area, I felt that an offer of $135,000 would be reasonable. I'd be getting the house at the low market price plus I'd have enough money left to fix it up. However, I also decided to use a broker. (I have a broker's license, but I was not eligible to buy the house and get a commission as well.)

The broker I used indicated that he knew of no other offers on the property and it had been out there for several weeks. He insisted that I was crazy to offer so much. "Why not make a low-ball offer? Why not offer $85,000? If you get it, you've gotten a steal." I was willing to pay $135,000 for the property. I could rent it out for PITI at that price. Nevertheless, I allowed myself to be tempted by his words. So I offered the $85,000.

As it turned out, the FHA official in charge decided simply not to sell. This was against the FHA's own directives in the area. Nevertheless, he was the person on the spot and he made the call. My offer was turned down. Disgusted both with the broker and myself for listening to him, I made the original $135,000 offer. However, by that time another buyer had come in and her offer was positioned ahead of mine. I lost out on the property.

I've often said that one of the reasons I feel confident in suggesting courses of action for investors to take is that at one time or another, I've already made most of the mistakes. This was a case in point.

If you're considering making a bid on an FHA repo, don't be greedy. Make your best offer and chances are you'll come out fine.

A Judgment Call

If there are a lot of FHA repos in your area, by all means consider them. They can provide an excellent means of obtaining a good rental property.

But, be aware of the pitfalls, many of which are noted in this chapter. Watch out for hopeless property. Be aware that you're going to have to come up with more cash than someone who intends living in the property. And don't get greedy.

Tip

___

The Veterans Administration (VA) also runs a repo program similar to that of the FHA, although much smaller. You don't have to be a veteran to buy a VA repo and sometimes there are real bargains to be had at close to or below market price. Call your local VA office to find out.

11
Financing Tricks for Investors

The words "nothing down" were made famous by Robert Allen in his real estate book of the same name. They came to symbolize the ultimate investment—you put nothing of your own in the pot, yet you ended up controlling property often worth hundreds of thousands of dollars.

The kicker, of course, was repayment. Yes, you could put nothing down. But unless you resold for a profit almost immediately, you could get killed with high monthly payments. That gave rise to another real estate bit of jargon, the "alligator." The alligator was a property you got for nothing down, or close to it, that then ate you alive with high payments.

In this book we're going to be more realistic. We're not going to look for nothing down properties and we're assiduously going to avoid alligators. Our strategy is to buy, rent, and *hold*. Holding means that the monthly payment has to be payable on a long-term basis. If it's too high and the rent doesn't cover it, your goose will be cooked long before the market turns and you have a chance to sell.

Therefore, the subject of this chapter might more appropriately be called, "something down." Yes, you're going to have to put something into the pot. That's the bad news. The good news, however, is that, with luck, the amount you put in will be relatively small and manageable.

Lender Discrimination

Lenders do discriminate against small investors in real estate. If you plan to occupy the house that you buy, one formula for determining the size of the mortgage is used. If you plan to rent it out, a different and stricter

113

formula is brought forth. In short, the down payments for investor-bought, nonoccupied houses are significantly higher.

This discrimination is totally unwarranted. While it is true that investor-bought *large* properties such as office buildings, apartment buildings, and commercial centers have frequently fallen into foreclosure and are responsible in large part for the savings and loan industry debacle, the same does not apply to small investors of single-family houses. I have seen no statistics that suggest that small investors (those who buy one or two properties) buying individual homes have defaulted at a rate higher than buyers who occupy the homes. Most statistics, in fact, suggest just the opposite. The investors tend to hang onto the properties through bad times while the occupant-owners more frequently bail out.

Government Discrimination

Nevertheless, the fact remains that if you plan to buy an investment property and not occupy it yourself, you will be discriminated against. This bias is widespread throughout the lending industry and is prescribed by government edict. (The government tells lenders what a large number of their policies will be. If they don't follow the rules, the government won't allow them to resell their mortgages on the secondary market, which it in effect controls.)

The discrimination takes two forms. The first is the down payment. As an investor, you will be required to come up with a substantially larger down payment. (As of this writing, owner-occupants can put down as little as 5 percent—investor nonoccupants are required to put up as much as 30 percent.)

The second form of discrimination is with regard to loan terms. The investor typically has to pay a higher interest rate (it's only very slightly higher since financial institutions realize that the risk really isn't there) and typically must pay full points and fees. Owner-occupants, besides paying a slightly lower interest rate, often are given breaks on the points and fees.

Avoiding Discrimination

There really is no way to avoid discrimination *as an investor.* You will be required to indicate on your loan application whether or not you intend to occupy the property. As soon as you write that you don't intend to occupy it (instead are planning to rent it out), you fall into the investor category and all the restrictions that go with it.

Trap

Never lie about your intention. Some investors have lied to lenders indicating that they intended to occupy the property when, in fact, they didn't. Since virtually all lenders do some government loans, the government investigates (through the Treasury Department or the FBI) any lying on loan applications. If you are discovered, the penalties can be quite severe.

However, if you *do* intend to occupy the property and you *do* in fact occupy it, you immediately come under the heading of owner-occupant and all the preferred treatment that offers. Therefore, my suggestion is to occupy the property for a time, if you can.

After all, you have to live somewhere. Why not buy a house to live in? After you've lived in it for awhile, perhaps 6 months or a year, move on to another house while renting the old one out.

In this way you can acquire investment properties with smaller down payments and more favorable terms. This is a tried and true method which has worked for countless small investors over the past 50 years.

Tip

Lenders are not ignorant to the ways of investors. Recently they have begun inserting clauses into their mortgages which state something to the effect that if you rent out the property, the mortgage immediately becomes due. In other words, you default on your mortgage if you stop living in the property and instead rent it out.

My own feeling is that lenders have put this in to satisfy government overseers. If the borrower, at a later date, defaults on the property and the lender has to take it back—and it turns out it was a rental instead of an owner-occupied dwelling—the lender can point to the clause and say that it did all that it could to ensure that the borrower did, indeed, occupy the premises.

To my knowledge, few lenders, if any, of purchase money mortgages have attempted to enforce this clause. If they did, I am sure there would be court challenges and it very well might prove to be illegal, depending on the state and the judge. (This clause, however, has been enforced in home equity loans where it is frequently found. Home equity loans, however, are not usually used to purchase a property.)

In any event, you should look for such a clause when you obtain a purchase money mortgage and you should be aware that even if you initially occupy the property, if you later rent it out, you could be placing yourself at risk.

How Much Down?

For the remainder of this chapter, we're going to deal with financing as
if you're an investor. However, here and there we'll also mention what
the terms are if you happen to be able to occupy the property.

The actual amount of the down payment you are required to make depends, to a great extent, on how you structure the deal. In today's market in a conventional financed deal (no FHA terms), as an investor you
can expect to be asked to put between 20 and 30 percent down (10 to 20
percent as an owner-occupant).

On a $100,000 property, the deal with conventional financing would
look like this:

Down	$20,000 to $30,000
Mortgage	$80,000 to $70,000
Purchase price	$100,000

Now, I'm not suggesting that you do this or that this is a great way to
structure a purchase. Most small investors, in fact, don't happen to have
$30,000 (plus closing costs) to plunk down on a property, particularly
when the market is as bad as it is today. Examining this basic deal is, however, a good starting point.

In a cold market the seller is very often willing (as noted earlier) to
help you make the purchase. Therefore, it is my suggestion that when
you make the offer, you insist that the seller help with the financing. In
other words, require a second mortgage from the seller. For example,
you may get a new first mortgage for 70 percent of the purchase price.
But, you can also insist on a second mortgage for 20 percent of the sales
price from the seller. A seller who is anxious to sell might very well give
you this and most lenders won't mind if a substantial part of the down
payment is in the form of a second mortgage.

Tip

Most lenders will balk if you put down less than 10 percent cash. You can
try it, but be aware that the deal may not fly.

Financing with a seller's second mortgage and conventional financing
would look like this:

Down	$ 10,000
Second	$ 20,000
Mortgage	$ 70,000
Purchase price	$100,000

By having the seller help with the financing, a much lower down payment is required. In addition, there could be other benefits. As of this writing, interest rates on a conventional first mortgage are hovering around 11 percent. If you go to any bank, savings and loan, or other institutional source, that's what you'll pay.

However, there is no set rate for seller financed seconds. As noted in Chapter 5, there is no reason why you can't ask for (demand) a lower interest rate on a second mortgage. For example, the second could be at 8 percent. The difference between 8 percent and 11 percent on a second mortgage of $20,000 over 10 years is about $35 a month. Not only will the seller save you the difficult task of coming up with $20,000 more in cash, but he or she can also offer you lower monthly payments.

Getting Seller Financing

This brings up the next possibility. What about having the seller finance the entire purchase instead of just giving a second mortgage? Couldn't you get an even lower down payment with a much lower monthly payment that way?

Yes, you can—except that most sellers cannot finance the sale of their property. Remember, in real estate almost no one owns property outright. Everyone has a mortgage. That includes the seller. He or she can't finance the total sale of the property because he or she needs cash to pay off an existing loan.

An Example

However, a seller can finance as much equity as is in a property. Let's consider the case of Teresa. Teresa had purchased her home nearly 20 years earlier for $40,000. Today she wanted to sell and even in a cold market, it was worth $120,000. However, she still owed $20,000 on her original mortgage, which was not assumable. She was planning to retire and she really didn't need a large bundle of cash. Instead, what she wanted was a kind of annuity. She wanted money coming in each month to pay her living expenses.

When Jonathan, an investor, came across Teresa, he saw an opportunity. He saw a way to give her what she wanted as well as to get a good deal for himself. He offered her this package, a seller financed deal:

Down	$ 12,000
Second	$ 88,000
First	$ 20,000
Purchase price	$120,000

He made the standard 10 percent down payment. However, he went to a lender for only $20,000. That was just enough to pay off the existing mortgage. His $20,000 new loan was at the going rate of 11 percent.

He then offered Teresa the second at 9 percent, 2 percent below the market rate. He made no secret that the 9 percent rate was low. However, he did point out how bad the market was and that this was really the only way he would buy the property.

From Teresa's viewpoint, the deal wasn't all that bad. She would get $12,000 in cash from the down payment which she could use to pay the commission and closing costs plus have some cash left over. In addition, she would get a monthly payment of roughly $800 (the mortgage was for 20 years) on which to live. She saw many benefits to the deal, and she took it.

From Jonathan's perspective, it was a good deal also. If he had been able to secure conventional financing for the $88,000 that Teresa was financing, his monthly payments would have been about $910 a month (again assuming a 20 year term). Handling it this way saved him more than $110 a month in payments. Of course, as an investor, he couldn't have gotten the full $88,000 in financing. As an investor without Teresa's help, he would have had to put as much as 30 percent down or an additional $24,000.

Is This a Realistic Deal?

I'm sure readers are wondering just how realistic this sort of a deal is. The answer is that it's not only realistic, it's done every day. The catch, the hard part, is to find a seller who has sufficient equity and who doesn't want to cash out. Most sellers today are not in this position. Most sellers have big mortgages and they need their equity out in the form of cash so that they can use it to buy another property.

Nevertheless, sellers such as Teresa do exist. You just have to look for them.

Tip

It's important to note that Jonathan could have structured the deal even more to his favor. He could have given Teresa nothing down and asked for a ridiculously low interest rate on the second, for example, 5 percent. If she had accepted, he would have gotten in with virtually no cash and have minimal monthly payments.

This, however, would have been a "rip-off" of Teresa in a variety of ways. Without at least 10 percent down, she wouldn't have any assurance that he would continue to make the payments on the house, if times got worse. Also, she wouldn't have any cash with which to pay the commission and her closing costs. His monthly payments might have been too low for her to live on. And finally, through a complicated set of IRS rulings, the government might have "imputed" a higher interest rate to her for tax purposes meaning that although she only received 5 percent actual interest, she might have had to pay taxes on the money as if she had received the market rate, or 11 percent. (Imputed interest is a very complex subject with many variables and a lot of judgment calls—check with your tax attorney or accountant for more information.)

While it's nice to assume Jonathan was such an upstanding individual and that he wouldn't have dreamed of ripping-off Teresa, the fact of the matter is that structuring a deal in the above way was in fact done by some unscrupulous characters in the early 1980s who were searching for low down deals.

As a result, the word got out and today's sellers and agents are far wiser than before. No seller in his or her right mind would accept the rip-off deal noted above and no real estate agent worth his or her salt would recommend it.

If you're thinking that maybe there are still unscrupulous people out there who might have sweetened the deal for themselves, keep in mind that they're not operating in a vacuum. Besides the fact that the authorities are always on the look out for rip-off artists, there's also the fact that other investors might slip in with a better deal for Teresa and the unscrupulous investor could lose out.

Down Payments of Less Than 10 Percent

As an investor, it's simply going to be very difficult to purchase an investment property with less than 10 percent down. No institutional lender will be willing to give you a mortgage with a smaller down payment and most will insist on much more. You can try banks, S&Ls, credit unions, and so forth, but the answer is going to be pretty much the same.

On the other hand, as noted earlier, if you can agree to occupy the property, the story is quite different. For owner-occupants, you can get in with as little as 5 percent down. Most lenders offer private mortgage insurance (PMI). PMI allows a down payment with a conventional mortgage of as little as 5 percent. However, in order to qualify you must have extraordinarily good credit, the property must be in top notch condition in a good location, and you'll have to pay an additional percentage for the PMI.

Tip
___

Be forewarned—if you do plan to be a buyer and an occupant and stroll into a lender and ask about PMI insured loans at 95 percent of the purchase price, you will get a lot of turn downs. They will be happy to talk with you at 90 percent. But at 95 they seem to forget how to speak. You may even be told that no such thing exists.

The truth is that lenders can only issue a small percentage of their portfolio in 95 percent mortgages, something like 5 or 10 percent, depending on the government's current regulations. In addition such loans fall into the highest risk category for the institution when it comes to calculating their capital requirements, which were made far stricter by Financial Institutions Reform, Recovery and Enforcement Act of 1989 (FIRREA). As a result, most institutions simply won't bother with the 5 percent down loans and those that do, don't advertise them. They are available, but you'll have to search hard.

Another alternative is the FHA program. You can get in with as little as 5 percent down here, too. However, as before, you must be an owner-occupant and the qualifying is very strict, plus you must pay the FHA insurance (roughly 0.5 percent of the loan) up front. Finally, the maximum FHA loan, as of this writing, is not much more than $125,000. Hence, in much of the country with high-priced property, this isn't a real possibility.

Deciding on the Best Types of Mortgages

For the remainder of this chapter we're going to look into the types of mortgages that are available to you, their pros and cons. You should be aware that today, like never before, the diversity of home mortgages is enormous. We won't be able to cover it all but will instead look at the most popular kinds that are useful to investors. For more information, I suggest you look into *Making Mortgages Work for You* (McGraw-Hill, 1987).

The Pros and Cons of Fixed-Rate Mortgages

This is the traditional mortgage that has been around since the end of the great depression. It is simply a mortgage with an interest rate fixed at the time you obtain it. For example, you might get a 30-year mortgage at a rate of 10.7 percent. At year 5 the rate will be 10.7 percent, as it will at year 10 and year 30. Regardless of what happens in the marketplace, this interest rate will not fluctuate.

Tip

Although I use the word "mortgage" generically, the more common loan instrument in real estate today is the trust deed. The trust deed is probably what you will get when you finance your investment property. It has three participants, a beneficiary (lender), a trustor (borrower), and a trustee who, in effect, holds the power to sell the property should you default on your payments.

The trust deed is in common use in most parts of the country. It is easier for a lender to make a loan with it and to get the property back if the borrower defaults. Don't be intimidated by it. But don't be lulled into thinking it has no teeth. It's always a good idea to have a a competent real estate attorney review your loan instruments before you sign.

In the past I have always favored the fixed-rate mortgage for the simple reason that you can't be undercut by it. You know up front what your interest rate will be and it doesn't vary. I can't think of the number of buyers who have purchased using an adjustable rate mortgage (discussed shortly) only to find after a few years that their monthly payments have moved up significantly. (An increase of 25 to 35 percent over 5 years is not uncommon.) This holds true for home buyer-occupants as well as investors. In my opinion, the adjustable rate mortgage has contributed more to the high foreclosure rate in this country than anything else.

Yet for today's investor, I'm no longer recommending the fixed-rate mortgage. Times and conditions have changed and a new strategy is called for.

The very strength of the fixed-rate mortgage, a predictable monthly payment is now its weakness, for investors. The reason is simple. When you buy, rent, and hold, very likely you don't intend to hold forever. (If holding indefinitely is your strategy, you may want to consider the fixed-rate mortgage again.)

Rather your goal is to hold only until the market turns around and prices move up. Then you want to sell. For that strategy, an adjustable rate mortgage may prove to be a better instrument because you will be able to take advantage of its lower initial rate.

The Pros and Cons of Adjustable Mortgages

In an adjustable mortgage the interest rate fluctuates. When you get the mortgage, you typically start out at a very low "teaser" rate. Then, over time, the rate (and the monthly payments) increase until you're paying the market rate. You may even have to play catch-up as interest rates subsequently fall, yet your monthly payments continue to rise to catch up to previously high rates. The rate adjusts (hence the name of the mortgage) at preset intervals such as every month or every 6 months or every year depending on an index. Typical indices include the cost of funds to the lender, Treasury bills, and an average of current fixed-rate mortgage rates.

There are many pitfalls to adjustable rate mortgages and we'll discuss some of them here. However, our main thrust is to consider this type of mortgage in light of a house investment. Where are the benefits?

The basic benefit of the adjustable rate mortgage comes from the fact that as an investor, presumably, you're not going to hang onto the property indefinitely. Rather, your intention is to hold only until the market turns around. If you can get a mortgage that, because it is adjustable, gives you a lower than market rate during the period of ownership, you've gotten a real benefit. Perhaps an illustration will help.

An Example. Rita found an investment house that was perfect. The price was right and it was in a strong tenant market. To make the deal work, however, she had to get low monthly payments.

The house price was $90,000. She planned on putting 20 percent down ($18,000) and obtaining a new first mortgage for $72,000. The trouble was that the current interest rate was 11 percent, which gave her a monthly payment (on a 30-year mortgage) of $686. When she added in costs for taxes and insurance, the total monthly payment came to around $900. However, the rental market in the area plateaued at about $800. She would lose $100 a month on a fixed-rate mortgage. (For this example, we're omitting calculations for maintenance costs, depreciation, and so forth.) Although $100 a month isn't a huge amount these days, it is $1200 a year and over a period of years, could add up. In addition there's the psychological effect of having to take extra money out of pocket each month to keep a property. It can't help but make you wonder if you have done the right thing.

What Rita needed to do was to get that monthly payment down closer to the anticipated rental income. One way was to get an adjustable-rate mortgage. Adjustables were offered in a wide variety of forms from all the local lending institutions. Rita investigated several of them until she found an adjustable with a starting rate of 9 percent. At 9 percent, her monthly mortgage payment was about $100 lower. Thus her rental income should just cover the PITI costs. Rita went for the adjustable mortgage.

Finding the Right Adjustable-Rate Mortgage

In this example, the lower initial rate of the adjustable mortgage allowed Rita to comfortably buy the property. However, it would be a mistake to think that adjustables are like Santa Claus or the Tooth Fairy. They don't just give benefits; they take penalties as well.

As noted earlier, the interest rate tends to rise above the initial rate. (That is why the initial rate is called the teaser. It teases you into thinking you're getting a lower overall rate than you really are.)

The reason the rate rises is that an adjustable mortgage, regardless of the index on which the rate is based, follows the same market as fixed-rate mortgages. If the real current interest rate for fixed mortgages is 10 percent, for example, it's also roughly 10 percent for adjustables. But, to entice you get the adjustable mortgage, the lender reduces the initial rate. But, over time that initial rate will rise until the real rate you are paying matches, roughly, the rate for fixed-rate mortgages.

If you plan to keep the property for the life of the loan, say 30 years, that initial low rate isn't going to make much difference. However, if as an investor you're only going to keep the property until the market turns around, you can use that initial teaser rate to your advantage.

The idea is to find an adjustable rate with a low teaser and with adjustments that keep that initial rate low for as long as possible. Although they are rarely available, what you would ideally like to find is an adjustable where the initial rate is low for 5 years. Then, after 5 years, you sell the property. That way you would be paying a lower than market rate during your entire term of ownership.

What to Look for in Adjustables

What you need to look for in an adjustable, besides a low initial rate, which is obvious, is for small adjustments and long adjustment periods.

Small Adjustments. Small adjustments mean that at each adjustment period the amount the rate can change is small, 1 percent or less. Ideally, you would like an adjustment that is limited to ½ percent or less. This way, the bumps will come in tiny increments.

Long Adjustment Periods. You are also looking for long adjustment periods. Some adjustable rate mortgages adjust every month. That's not for you. If the rate adjusts half a percentage point each month and the initial rate is 3 percent below market, in just 6 months you could be back up to the market rate (assuming interest rates didn't go up or down during that period).

What you want are adjustment periods of 6 months or longer. Some adjustables don't change their rates over 12 months. That's even better. Some change every 3 years, which, depending on the other terms, could be better still.

The idea is to calculate your sale horizon. When do you reasonably expect the market to turn around so you can sell for profit? Then add a bit more time for a margin of error and use that amount to determine your ideal adjustable rate mortgage. For example, if you figure you won't be able to pull your profits out for 5 years, try to find an adjustable that gives you benefits for nearly that long.

Adjustables in the Real World

Lenders, of course, are well aware of the fact that buyers will try to stretch out the teaser rate as long as possible. They know that it's to their advantage to make the time for the teaser rate as *short* as possible. Hence, your interests are exactly opposite of the lenders. Nevertheless, there may be some room for maneuverability.

In the real world, the rule of thumb is that the adjustable with the *lowest teaser rate* also has the shortest adjustment periods and the highest adjustments. For example, if you find an adjustable rate mortgage at 6 percent at a time when the market rate is 11 percent (a five-point spread), you can bet the farm that the adjustment periods are going to be monthly and the rate of adjustment will be high, perhaps 2 percent each period.

Yes, you'll get a very low teaser rate. But within 3 months, you'll be back up to the market rate. Reality will set in very quickly. Quite frankly, these adjustables with very low teaser rates and rapid and big adjustments are for suckers. They also contribute significantly to foreclosures when unwary borrowers suddenly find their monthly mortgage payments increasing by a third or more.

On the other hand, adjustables with less spread between the teaser rate and current market rate tend to have longer adjustment periods and smaller adjustments. For example, you might find an adjustable at 9 percent when the current market for mortgage is at 11 percent, just a 2 percent spread.

But the adjustment period might be annual and the adjustment rate only one-half of 1 percent. With this mortgage it would take you 4 years to get up to the current market rate. During that period rents might conceivably rise and your PITI might never get above your rental rate.

Thus, what you're looking for is not the lowest initial rate but the best combination of rate, adjustment period, and adjustment rate.

Choosing from Among Hundreds of Adjustable Possibilities

You will find that the types of adjustable mortgages available to you are simply staggering in their diversity. For example, I recently made a survey of the different types of adjustable-rate mortgage available on the West Coast. I came up with over a hundred. Of course, there were many similarities. But, at the same time, there were many differences. Below are a few of these that we haven't yet discussed and the possible benefits to you.

Convertible Mortgage. Here the adjustable is converted to a fixed rate. Typically you start out with an adjustable and then, at a set time, perhaps after 5 or 7 years, you can convert the loan to a fixed rate. Sometimes the conversion period is over several years, for example, after 3 but not longer than 10 years after you get the mortgage.

As an investor, a convertible is of no particular advantage to you, unless fixed rates happen to crash just at the time of the conversion (most unlikely, but possible). The problem with convertibles is that for the privilege of converting at a later date, you usually get a lower teaser rate and less favorable adjustment periods and rates. That's a lot to give up when you plan to sell the property anyway, perhaps before the convertible date occurs.

Bimonthly Mortgage. With a bimonthly mortgage you pay every other week instead of monthly. Since there are 52 weeks in the year but only 12 months, at the end of the year you've made an extra mortgage payment. Over the life of the mortgage, paying an extra payment could save you tens of thousands of dollars in interest, perhaps hundreds of thousands depending on the size of the mortgage.

For you as an investor, however, there is no advantage here. You're not planning to keep the property for the life of the mortgage. You're only planning to keep it until you can resell it.

There's even a disadvantage. Having to make an extra payment each year will surely mean you won't recoup your expenses from your rent. Try telling a tenant that he or she has to make an extra payment each year because you've got a bimonthly mortgage.

Capped Monthly Payment. In this mortgage there is a cap placed on the monthly payment. It can't rise above a certain amount. For example, no matter how high interest rates may go, the cap can't move upward beyond a certain point.

Usually this type of mortgage is a "no-no." It results in "negative amortization," which means that the interest which you don't pay because of a cap on your monthly payment is added to the mortgage amount. In other words, instead of your mortgage going down, it goes up.

For someone who plans to hold the house over a long period of time, this is the worst possible kind of mortgage. But for you as an investor, it holds certain benefits. (Of course, if interest rates plummet dramatically, you are really sitting pretty. Your adjustable-rate mortgage payments might never go up. Instead, they could actually go down.)

The benefits of the capped monthly payment is that you don't have a big worry about mortgage payments getting out of line with rental income. Interest rates could surge, yet you're locked into a low monthly payment. This could bring real peace of mind when it comes to those sleepless nights spent worrying about taking money out of your pocket to make the investment house mortgage.

But what about the negative amortization? Don't worry about it. Your goal is to sell for large profits. So what if they won't be quite so large when you have to pay back the negative amortization. If all goes well, they should be more than enough to offset the negative. (If they're not and you have to hold the property longer than you anticipated, the lower monthly payments will still benefit you.)

Admittedly this is a risky outlook. But then, if you're not a risk-taker, you don't belong in this business.

Tip

The way the government rules were written (and they are subject to change), a mortgage can never exceed the original appraised value of the property. For example, if you get an 80 percent loan, the negative amortization can never exceed 100 percent of the original appraised value. If the appraisal was $100,000 and your mortgage was $80,000, the maximum negative amortization you can get is $20,000. This can be some comfort to you. Although a 20 percent increase is substantial, it isn't the end of the world. (*Note*: This applies only to mortgages which are in some way involved with the federal government. Nearly all "firsts" fit into this category.)

The Bottom Line

The long and the short of it is that the financing you get is critical. Get the right financing and it can not only help make the deal work, it can also make it easier to sustain the property while you're holding it. Get the wrong financing, and you're in trouble.

12
Tips for Aggressive Renting

An Investment in Time

The key to success in any business is minding the store. Whether it's a fast food outlet or retail sales, whether you're selling insurance or ice cream cones, you've got to be on top of the business all the time. To be successful, you can't be out lying in the sun in Palm Springs when something needs to be done. You've got to be there to do it. The same holds true of renting property.

Because rentals do not take up a lot of time, many first time landlords think that they don't require *any* time. That's simply not so. You may go months without a rental problem. But when one occurs, you've got to be "Johnny on the spot" to solve it, or else you'll lose rental income or significantly increase your costs.

In this chapter we're going to talk about aggressive renting. The term "aggressive" may throw some readers off. No, we're not talking about taking advantage of tenants. What we're talking about here is not letting tenants take advantage of you. This chapter will discuss how to get your rental income delivered promptly to you each month with a minimum of hassle.

Choosing Quality Tenants

I've been a landlord for over 30 years. I've rented residential property (from large apartment complexes down to single-family units) both for others as a broker and for myself. During that time I've had very few bad tenants. I would say that better than 97 percent of the tenants that I've had have paid all the rent that was due and left the property in acceptable shape.

My philosophy is that if I pick the right tenant in the beginning, things will work out in the end. A good tenant wants to pay the rent, on time, and wants to take care of the property. My job simply becomes allowing that tenant to do what comes natural.

I'm sure that some readers who have had bad tenant experiences are shaking their head. It may all sound like "pie in the sky" to them. Maybe. But, over the years I've developed some tips which have helped me out enormously. This is not to say that I haven't had some bad experiences. I have. But I have been able to hold them to a minimum. I hope these tips will work for you.

Tip 1—Get Your Head Straight

Some have written that we Americans share collective feelings of guilt about the downtrodden. Perhaps it comes from our massacre of the Native Americans who originally ruled this land, perhaps from our country's early shameful experience with slavery. (It helps to remember that the Native Americans we displaced in many cases themselves previously displaced other tribes.) In any event, this collective guilt sometimes surfaces when we first become landlords. After all, the word itself means "lord of the land." That suggests that the tenant is the servant of the landlord.

Something we Americans abhor is the notion of servitude. As a result I have seen first time landlords bend over backward to cater to the whims of their tenants. They accept late rents and provide unreasonable services all in the desire to prove that they are not superior to their tenants. In short they go out of their way to make their tenants feel equal. Along the way they stop renting aggressively and usually end up paying for it financially.

A Position of Risk and Responsibility

The truth is that the landlord is in a much more financially responsible position than the tenant. As landlord you own the property. You stand to reap all the profits if values go up and to lose a significant amount of money if they go down. You also have all the responsibilities of paying taxes, insurance, mortgage interest, as well as repairs. The tenant has none of those responsibilities. He or she only has to get the rent in on time and keep the place reasonably clean and tidy.

Because of the different responsibilities, you can never be on the same level as the tenant. The property is always going to mean more to you than to the tenant. And you are always going to have to be in the position of having to dictate terms to the tenant.

Striking a Businesslike Tone

In short, renting property is not democracy in action. It's more like a monarchy. You're more like a king and the tenant is more like a subject. While this analogy is helpful, it's important not to stretch it too far. In the old days (meaning more than 50 years ago), landlords tended to act dictatorially. In some states there are still self-help evictions on the law books. Although virtually never used today, a self-help eviction means if the landlord determines that the tenant isn't paying rent, he or she personally can throw the tenant's possessions onto the street and physically drag the tenant out of the property. (Yes, this used to be the rule more than the exception through the early days of this century.)

To counter unfair treatment by some landlords, the courts over the years strengthened tenants' rights to the point where today many landlords feel the tenants have the upper hand. In most states the landlord is so restricted in what he or she can and cannot do that some people say it just isn't worth renting out property any more. I don't find that to be true. To my way of thinking the courts and the legislatures have simply given tenants protections that they needed from unscrupulous landlords. If you're not unscrupulous, you should have little to worry about.

The whole point of this discussion is to note the importance of striking the right tone in your relationship with a tenant. You can't be arbitrary or dictatorial. Yet, you can't be a wimp, either. You have to be in charge. It's your property and how you handle the tenant will largely determine what happens to it. Get your head straight. The tenant is not doing you a favor by renting from you—he or she needs shelter and has to rent from someone. On the other hand, you're not doing the tenant a favor—there are lots of other rentals.

Remember, it's a business and should be run as such. You're the boss, and within the law, you set up the rules and see that they are followed. Keep to that thinking and you should do well.

Important Note: It's vital that you pick up a set of landlord and tenant laws appropriate to your state and study it before you begin renting. While the rules may differ from state to state, in almost all cases they are plain and you don't want to break them. A tenant lawsuit is no fun for anyone.

Tip 2—Rent a Clean Property

The Case against Dirt

The Biblical observation, "As you sow, so shall you reap" really does apply here. If the property you rent is clean when the tenant moves in, the chances are very good it will be clean when the tenant moves out.

This should be obvious, but it really isn't. I have known many landlords who really don't care what their property looks like. Their attitude seems to be, "I'm not going to live there, so what do I care? Let the tenants clean it if they want. They're all a bunch of pigs anyway."

That's not a very charitable attitude and it often comes from having a tenant who leaves the property a mess. However, having once been burned does not mean you need to fear fire. (It was Mark Twain who observed that a cat that jumps on a hot stove will never jump on a hot one again, or a cold one either, for that matter.)

Dirty and messy properties take far longer to rent, command lower rents, and attract a much lower-quality tenant. The person you really hurt when you fail to clean up your rental is you. I always go through a rental and clean the carpets and floors, make sure the kitchen is spotless with the stove, refrigerator (if any), and the sink shiny and clean. I also repaint the walls as necessary. When prospective tenants walk in, I want them to think they are getting a place that's as good as new. That way, they are more likely to take pride in living there and will take care of it.

Do-It-Yourself versus
Tenant-Initiated Cleanup

One special note: Sometimes when a property has a lot of tenants moving through it, it begins to take on a shabby appearance. After awhile the landlord tires of spending the money and time to clean it after each tenant and instead, offers to pay for the paint and cleaning equipment if the tenant will do the cleanup work.

My experience is that this works only in a very limited way. If the property is already cleaned up, but a little bit on the worn side and the tenant wants a gallon of paint to touch up a bedroom, by all means buy the paint. You probably have a very clean tenant who will take good care of the property. On the other hand, if the place is a mess and the tenant wants a gallon of paint to fix it up, don't buy the paint. Have the place fixed up before you go looking for a tenant.

I've tried it both ways and I've found that tenants who are willing to rent a place that is a mess, even if they are willing to clean it up a bit, will still turn out to be poor-quality tenants who have trouble making rent payments and who leave the place even worse.

A good tenant simply won't accept a rental that's a mess. He or she won't want to spend much time (with the occasional exception of the fastidious tenant noted above) cleaning. They know they are good tenants, they know they can find a clean place, and they will skip yours. As a result, you get what's left—the type of tenant you don't want.

Note: If you do buy paint for the tenant or otherwise allow them to fix up the place, be sure that you choose the paint, wallpaper, or whatever. Always select the best possible quality (so it will last) and the most generic colors (so they will appeal to the most people). If you let the tenant make the selection, you could end up with a purple bathroom and red living room.

Tip 3—Provide an Allowance for Water, if Applicable

In most rentals the tenant pays the utility bills. This includes gas or oil, electricity, phone, and water. This is almost certainly the case with single-family residences where everything is separately metered.

There's nothing wrong with this, unless you live in an arid climate and have a lot of landscaping. That landscaping will take water and in arid climates, water tends to be expensive. Don't expect any tenant to go out of his or her way to pay a big water bill to help *your* landscaping. Yes, most tenants do like nice landscaping. No, most tenants won't pay extra for it.

The answer is a water allowance. It doesn't have to be much. It doesn't even have to equal the costs the tenant will pay for water actually used. It's just the idea that you're contributing. Each time the tenant thinks about not watering, he or she will remember that allowance, will not get angry about the cost, and will water.

It doesn't work for every tenant, but it does work for many and it could save you a lot of costs in relandscaping later on.

Note: If you have large yards in front and back, you may want to consider providing a gardener. You often can charge more rent with a gardener, so there could be almost no cost to you and it can mean keeping the property in great shape. If the property has a pool, a pool maintenance service is a must. Never rely on a tenant to take care of a pool.

Tip 4—Qualify Your
Prospective Tenants Carefully

As suggested earlier, the way to get a tenant to take care of the property and pay the rent on time is to rent to the right tenant in the beginning. This is the biggest problem area for most new landlords—getting the right tenant. How do you do it? Rest assured there is no guaranteed formula. There are, however, certain tips which will prove helpful.

Of course you will want to talk with the prospective tenants and form an opinion of them. (This is very important and why I always suggest that you do the renting of the property personally.) I'll have more to say about this later in this section. For now, let's consider two other items which you will want to pay particular attention to after you've decided that the prospective tenants are likely candidates.

Obtaining a Credit Report

Today, you as a landlord should have no trouble in getting a written credit report on a prospective tenant. All that you really need to do is to contact one of the three or four credit agencies (listed in your phone book), explain what you want, and have them send you some of their forms. The cost is usually under $15 for a brief report.

When you find likely tenant candidates, have them fill out the form. Usually within a day you'll have a printout of their credit history. Check it over carefully. Ideally you're looking for tenants with no bad credit. They pay all their bills on time and have credit with a wide variety of lenders from credit card companies to department stores to banks. Chances are, however, you won't find this kind of tenant all the time (or even very often). More likely the person who rents has spotty credit, some good, some bad.

Study the credit report. If the prospective tenants have a lot of "late paying" notes, chances are your rent won't be paid on time, either. If they have some loan defaults or other failures to pay, you may not get your rent at all.

The credit report should be taken as an indication of how the prospective tenants view their credit. If they view it casually and don't really care, you could end up with no rent. You want tenants who take their credit seriously and who regularly pay on time. One of the biggest mistakes is to "fall in love" with a tenant (not literally, but figuratively). The tenant seems ideal, until the credit report comes in. You look at the bad credit report and then choose to ignore it because you're so convinced the tenant is wonderful. Bad move.

Ultimately it's a judgment call. Just remember, however, that if you didn't think the tenant's credit was an important indicator, why did you order the credit report in the first place?

Note: Always give the tenant a chance to explain bad credit. Listen to the explanation. It may be perfectly logical and may not be the tenant's fault.

Obtain Recommendations from Previous Landlords

To me this is the single most important indicator of future tenant success. It's absolutely vital that you get the accurate name and phone number of the tenants' former landlords. *It's a must that you get not just the previous landlord but those going back two or three rentals.* (If you just ask for the previous landlord, you might get the number of a brother-in-law or other family member or friend who gives you a wonderful recommendation. This is much harder to do with earlier landlords.)

Call up the former landlords and ask them about the tenant. Explain that you are planning to rent your property to this tenant. Ask for a recommendation.

Some landlords are pleased to tell you all they know. Others are hesitant to talk for fear that anything they say may later be used against them by the tenant. (Just as in employer-employee relationships, there have been cases where tenants have sued former landlords over bad recommendations.)

If the landlord is hesitant to volunteer information, you can ask questions that will get you the answers you want. For example:

Would you rerent to this tenant? Why not?

Would you charge a higher cleaning or security deposit next time? Why?

Would you allow this tenant to have a pet?

In nearly all cases you can quickly find out what you need to know from the former landlord. Listen carefully to what's said. Usually the former landlord has no axe to grind, unless the tenant skipped without paying rent. Then the landlord may bend your ear telling you what a turkey the tenant was.

The credit report and former landlord recommendations are the two best sources of information about your prospective tenants. Don't skip either. They are important.

Some Personal Experiences

Having given you the rules about credit reports and former landlord's recommendations, let me say that I've broken them as well as kept them. I've rented to tenants with horrific credit reports. And I've rented to tenants whose former landlords told horror stories about them.

Why? A lot has to do with gut feelings and the tenants' explanations. In one case I rented to a tenant who explained that her bad credit was due to a boyfriend who left her with a lot of bills. It turned out to be the truth and she was a great tenant. In another case I rented to a tenant whose former landlord said he left the place a mess with real damage done and never paid the rent on time. The tenant explained that he left it clean, paid the rent on time, but the former landlord was mad because he moved out over a dispute over painting. The former landlord had promised to repaint the insides of the house and reneged. I believed the tenant and again, he turned out great.

As I said, it's a judgment call.

Tip 5—Allow Children and Pets

How Many Children?

This seems to fly in the face of advice that most landlords give. They say avoid renting to children whenever possible and avoid pets like the plague. Both can do immense damage to property.

That certainly is true. On the other hand, the most reliable tenants tend to be the ones with kids. Family people tend to take care of property and pay the rent on time. If you try to avoid renting to kids, you may eliminate your best source of tenants.

Instead of not taking kids, try to rent to people who don't have more kids than the house can hold. A three bedroom, two bath house can easily accommodate two or three kids. It will, however, show wear and tear with six kids. Limit the number of children in the rental agreement. (Also, be aware that small children are sometimes terrible tenants since they tend to write on the walls in crayon, which won't come off and is very difficult to paint over.)

Note: *In some states it is illegal to deny a rental to a prospective tenant solely on the basis of that tenant's having children. Check the laws in your state.*

What About Pets?

In the case of dogs, I follow the philosophy of an old friend who manages over 150 single-family residences. He says,

People always lie about dogs. They always say they don't have any and then, once they move in, the dog appears. So what's the point of saying no dogs in the rental agreement? Are you going to throw out a good tenant because he or she "acquires" a dog?

Sometimes people come right out and say they have a dog. If I say no dogs, they say they'll get rid of the pet. I would never rent to anyone who would get rid of a pet.

As a result, I simply say that one dog is okay. If there end up being two, I look the other way. If there's a kennel, of course, I throw them out.

Cats and birds are something else. Cats which are not properly house trained may urinate on carpets. Cat urine is virtually impossible to get out. It may result in the need to get new padding under the carpeting, new carpets themselves, or even new flooring under the padding and the carpet. I always think twice before renting to a tenant with cats.

Birds can make a mess and they can leave a peculiar odor in the house which is hard, but not impossible, to remove. I also think twice about renting to a tenant with birds.

Tip 6—Never Get First and Last Month's Rent

This must certainly fly in the face of advice that most people have received. The lease in which a landlord gets first and last month's rent has been the traditional rental agreement. To now suggest that a landlord not go for it might be tantamount to criticizing mom, baseball, and apple pie. Yet, my advice is not to go for first and last month's rent. Here's why.

The traditional lease in which the tenant pays first and last month's rent grew mainly out of commercial usage. It's the sort of agreement you would use if you were renting a building to a commercial tenant. If the tenant didn't pay the rent on time, you could sue to collect the rent and you would always be 1 month ahead by collecting that last month's rent up front.

With a single house, however, realistically you're never going to sue to collect rent from a tenant who is in the premises and who isn't paying. You're simply going to want to get that tenant out and someone better in. Suing is the last thing you want to do. (You'll sue for unlawful detainer when the tenant doesn't leave and doesn't pay—and you might hope to recoup the lost rent later as a result of that suit.)

There's another problem with first and last month's rent. What you are mainly interested in (besides collecting rent) is that the tenant leave the property in as good a shape as he or she found it. First and last month's rent doesn't address that issue, a security and cleaning deposit does. Yet, if you've already collected first and last month's rent, how large a security deposit can you realistically hope to get? For example, if the rent is a $1000 a month, first and last month's rent comes to $2000. How much more can you expect a tenant to pay for a security deposit? $200? $500? You reach a point where your property requires too much cash up front for any likely tenant to afford.

A better way is to forego the last month's rent paid in advance and instead get a very large security and cleaning deposit. Today most savvy landlords are insisting on a security deposit at least equal to 1 month's rent if not more. If the property rents for $1000 a month, before moving in the tenant would be required to come up with $1000 for the first month's rent plus at least another $1000 or $1500 for a security deposit.

The tenant that puts up that much money has something substantial to lose if the property isn't left clean. And if the tenant doesn't pay, the deposit can always be used to compensate for lost rent. A last month's rent cannot be used as a cleaning deposit. (Check with the laws in your state to be sure that security deposits can be combined with cleaning deposits and used for either reason.)

One concern is the savvy tenant who doesn't make the last month's rent payment. When you call, the tenant says, please use the security and cleaning deposit.

You can write in the rental agreement that the cleaning and security deposit is *not* to be used as the last month's rent. You can argue until you're blue in the face. But the savvy tenant knows that it will take you more than a month to evict him or her and cost you a lot more than the security deposit, so that in the end, if they use it as the last month's rent, there's not a whole lot you can do.

Note: If you're concerned about an imminent market turnaround, go for a short-term lease, say six months. Remember that any sale is going to be subject to a tenant's lease rights. Alternatively, you could rent month-to-month, have the new buyer keep renting to the tenants until their lease is up; or, in the worst case, buy out the tenant's lease.

Note: Some states are now requiring landlords, even landlords of single-family residences, to keep security and cleaning deposits in a separate account and to pay the tenant interest on it. Check with the laws in your state.

Note Also: You may "lease" the property for a set period of time without getting the last month's rent. Getting the first month's rent plus a security deposit does not necessarily mean you are limited to month-to-month tenancy.

Tip 7—Try to Rent Just a Bit Lower than the Market

It's important not to be penny wise and pound foolish when you rent. The foolish landlord tries to get top dollar for a property. The wise landlord rents for just below the market.

The reasoning is simple—to get top dollar you have to wait for a tenant. If you rent just below the market, your property will always be full.

But, some newcomers to renting may ask, aren't you losing money that way? *Consider*: You're renting a house where the market for a property such as yours is $1000 a month. So you put your property up for $970. You'll lose $30 a month because you're renting below market. At the end of a year it will mean a loss of $360.

On the other hand, you'll rent up immediately. All else being equal, tenants will choose your property first over similar properties renting at $1000. Your property will be full all the time. (It's the same as when you go into the supermarket and see two products of equal quality next to each other—don't you buy the one that's 5 cents less than the other even though the price difference is negligible? Tenants act the same way.)

Now consider the landlords who insist on $1000 a month. Assuming that the market value is correct, they will get it. But, it might take them a month until they find a tenant, which will mean a loss of $1000 of potential rent during that month. Is it better to lose $360 or $1000?

But, some readers may ask, you'll keep losing money year after year. After awhile the other landlords have a better deal because they are charging more.

Not at all. At the end of the year, if you have a strong tenant who wants to stay and who you want to keep, raise your rent to the market level. If it's still $1000, raise it to that point. The tenant shouldn't want to move because, after all, you've just adjusted the rent to the true market value. Besides, moving is a terrible hassle and no one wants to do it for a savings of $30 a month.

On the other hand, your competitors who started at the higher price can't raise rents because they would then be *above* the market.

What we're talking about here is the rent-up period. You want to get your property rented fast because every day it's vacant costs you money. Renting just below the market will accomplish this.

Tip 8—Get a Penalty for Late Payment

This sometimes works for tenants who are always late. In any event it's a good idea to include it in every rental agreement you write. The penalty typically takes this form: In the rental agreement you include a clause which states words to the effect that if the tenant does not get the rent in by a certain number of days after the due date (typically 5 days grace is given), there is a penalty. The penalty is usually $50 or 5 percent of the rent, whichever is smaller.

This rent penalty is no more enforceable than the overall rental contract (meaning that you have to go to court to get enforcement, which you would most likely not do over $50). Nevertheless, in this modern world we are all conditioned to watch out for money penalties and tenants are no different. You'd be surprised how careful they will be to get the rent in on time to avoid the penalty.

One caution—you have to enforce the clause. If the rent is late and does not contain the $50, you may want to refuse to accept the rent until the $50 is paid. This runs the risk of not getting any rent, but if the ploy works, the tenant probably will pay on time ever after.

A version of this works well with tenants who are already in the premises, who do not have such a clause in their lease, and who begin paying later and later each month. This is the rent discount. What you do is raise the rent for this tenant. Very carefully you explain that it's been so long since you've raised the rent, that your costs have gone up and so forth and, in conclusion, you feel that a $50 a month rent increase is warranted to take effect immediately (or upon termination of the current lease).

However, if the tenant gets the rent in on time, there will be a $50 discount. In other words, the rent may be $1050. However, if the rent is delivered on time, it is reduced to $1000. You'll be surprised how many tenants will work hard to get that rent in when due.

Tip 9—Fix It Fast

I have a friend who is a most unlikely candidate for a landlord. He is self-centered, quick tempered, and obese (making it difficult for him to do any physical labor). Yet, he bought a rental house.

He succeeded in finding a tenant. However, within the first month the tenant called up early one evening to complain that the toilet wouldn't stop running. My friend swore at the tenant for disturbing his dinner and told the luckless fellow to fix the *@&% toilet himself. Needless to say, the tenant moved out the next month. After a few more such experiences, my friend sold the rental house—at a loss.

When you become a landlord you also assume the duties of a "fix-it person." You are expected to take care of all the little as well as all the big things that go wrong. This includes fixing leaky toilets and plugged drains, sprinkler systems that don't turn on, and light switches that don't turn off. What's more, you're expected to fix these things *quickly.*

While you might put up with a leaky toilet for weeks, a tenant who feels he or she is paying big bucks for the property won't put up with this at all. When they want things fixed, they want them fixed yesterday. If you don't respond and at least make the attempt to promptly correct the situation, you could lose your tenant. (Some states allow tenants to correct defective situations themselves and then deduct the cost from the rent. This is a definite no-no as far as you are concerned. The tenant might hire a plumber to fix a faucet and it would cost you $100, while you could have fixed it yourself for the cost of a 35-cent washer.)

If you can't fix things yourself, get the services of a someone who can. Rest assured there will always be something to fix and it's important to fix it fast.

Tip 10—Check Up
Once a Month

A rental property is a valuable asset. You may have hundreds of thousands of dollars invested in it. You've given it up to someone to live in for several hundreds of dollars a month. But that doesn't mean they are going to look after that asset as you would. Therefore, check up on your property. Don't wait until the tenant doesn't pay. Check up at least once a month.

Of course, you don't want to make a pest of yourself. Your rental agreement should give you the right to inspect the inside of the house with reasonable notice. But don't always bother a tenant who's paying the rent and keeping the place in good shape. Just driving by once and awhile can be enough.

When you see those lawns start turning brown and the flowers in front drying up, you know you've got a problem. Stop by and check it out. It's better to find out early that your tenant lost his or her job than later. Maybe you can help that tenant find another job or, at the least, another lower-cost rental.

Don't let things slip. You're the one who will get hurt in the long run.

Tip 11—Stay on Top of
Late Payments

The worst scenario is when the tenant won't pay and won't quit the property. We'll discuss that next. Here, we're concerned with the next to worst scenario—the tenant who is late in making payments. We already discussed one technique, the discount for timely payments. However, what do you do if the tenant is still late?

This is another judgment call. Definitely speak to the tenant. Find out what the problem is. Maybe the tenant is waiting for a check to come in. If the late payment happens infrequently and there's a good reason, perhaps it's best to overlook it.

But what if the tenant is very late, 1 week, 2 weeks late? Remember, your security and cleaning deposit is typically only equal to 1 month's rent. If the tenant is 2 weeks late, he or she has already used up half the security amount. Another 2 weeks and it's gone. Plus, if you have to evict, there's another month or two lost.

Most savvy landlords don't accept any late rent, not 1 day late. If it's 1 day late, they call or check with the tenant to see what the problem is. With a good tenant, it's usually an oversight and after that the rent's right on time. With a bad tenant, it's excuses.

If the rent is more than 3 days late without sufficient explanation, savvy landlords begin eviction. This usually means sending the tenant a legal notice (which you can get from any broker or most stationery stores and easily fill out yourself) demanding that the rent be paid or the tenant quit the premises. One such notice is usually sufficient to convince a tenant that you mean business.

If the tenant refuses to pay after 2 weeks, most savvy landlords begin eviction (discussed next). *Note:* waiting 2 weeks really doesn't cost you anything since most courts won't consider an unlawful detainer action until the tenant is at least 2 weeks late in rent.

The above time limits, however, are not set in stone. As with most things in renting property, it's a judgment call. On the one hand you don't want to scare, embarrass, or anger a good tenant into leaving just because 1 month they happened to overlook the rental due date. On the other hand, you don't want to give a bad tenant any more time than is absolutely necessary.

As I said, there is no one set answer. You have to play each case on its own merits. For myself, however, I would never let a tenant go more than 2 weeks without paying the rent no matter what the situation or how good I thought the tenant was. There's just too much at stake for me to lose.

Tip 12—Work with an Attorney for Eviction

Finally, you may at some time in your career as a landlord need to evict a tenant who won't pay the rent and who won't quit the premises. Remember, self-help is no longer allowed (except in some very few rural areas). Now you need the help of an eviction attorney.

Don't call just any attorney. Check around with local brokers, particularly those who handle property management. Usually there's one attorney in town who does nothing but evictions. Call him or her. This attorney undoubtedly already has set fees and knows the ropes. This attorney can get the tenant out with a minimum amount of cost and time to you.

In addition be sure that the attorney gets a judgment against the tenant for back rent owed. Often the attorney, or his or her investigators, can follow the former tenant to a new location and a new job and garnish wages to recoup your back rent. Usually their costs and fees are not deducted from the rent owed you. You may eventually get back everything you are owed. (Don't count on that happening every time, however.)

By the way, just getting the unlawful detainer judgment and eviction notice doesn't do it. You have to pay the sheriff to throw the tenant out, although even the worst tenants will usually voluntarily leave once they realize that the sheriff is coming.

Note: When a tenant doesn't pay and won't quit, be prepared for a loss. Chances are you'll lose some rent, at least the rent until the tenant is evicted. You'll probably also get the place back in a mess, so there will be clean up costs.

Note Also: Some tenants cannot be evicted. In some states a tenant who is in the last stages of pregnancy or is seriously ill and can provide a doctor's letter that he or she cannot be moved, may be allowed to stay in the property—at your expense. A tenant involved in bankruptcy may make the eviction proceedings part of the bankruptcy and postpone eviction. If you stay a landlord long enough, you'll see all kinds of problems.

The bottom line, however, is that while all sorts of problems can happen, they happen rarely. You may rent property all your life and never run into half the problems we've discussed in this chapter. But if you do, you now know how to handle them.

13
How to Save on Taxes

Owning residential real estate may offer you certain tax advantages, which could lower the personal income tax that you pay each year. However, a determination of whether you qualify for real estate tax advantages involves applying complex rules and decisions. It should not be made lightly. The purpose of this chapter is to provide an overview of federal taxation as it applies to real estate. This chapter should not be substituted for specific tax advice from a qualified practitioner. Before making any decisions involving tax consequences, you should seek advice from a competent accountant or tax attorney. In addition, material in this chapter reflects tax information *as of this writing*. It's important to keep in mind that subsequent changes or interpretations of the tax law could significantly affect the material that follows.

Passive versus Active

In 1986, the Tax Reform Act made changes to the way real estate is handled for tax purposes. These changes in general made it impossible in many cases to *write off* (deduct) losses against your ordinary income. There is one big exception that we'll get to shortly, but first, let's make sure that we understand what a write-off is.

In the past, owners of real estate could deduct from their personal income any losses they incurred on their property while renting it. Let's take an example. You own a rental house and over the course of the year you have the following income and expense statement.

Income and Expenses on a Rental Property

Expenses		Rental Income ($1000 monthly)
Mortgage	$ 9,000	
Taxes	1,300	
Insurance	500	
Maintenance	1,000	
Other	200	
Total out of pocket	12,000	
Depreciation	4,000	
Total expenses	−16,000	$12,000
Net loss	$ 4,000	

Your rental income of $12,000 just covers your out-of-pocket expenses. In short, your property is a wash—it is paying for itself. However, when depreciation is added in, you show a $4000 loss. (Depreciation is an allowance taken each year to compensate for the gradual loss in value of the property as it gets old and deteriorates. It is taken on the house only, not the land.)

Under the old tax laws, you could now deduct that $4000 loss (which is not out of pocket but which only appears on paper) from your personal income taxes, thus reducing them significantly. This ability to write off money that you didn't actually spend used to be one of the big tax advantages of owning property. That changed with the Tax Reform Act of 1986. Here's the gist of the new law as it affects real estate.

Active income. The tax law discriminates between the types of income that we receive. Income from wages or as compensation for services is called *active income.* It includes commissions, consulting fees, salary, or anything similar. It's important for those involved in real estate to note that profits and losses from businesses in which you "materially participate" (limited partnerships are not included) are included. *However, activities from real estate are specifically excluded.*

Passive income. This is a bit trickier to define, but in general it means the profit or loss that we receive from a business activity in which we *do not* materially participate. This includes not only limited partnerships but also income from any real estate that is rented out. It's important to note that real estate is *specifically defined* as passive.

Portfolio income. This is income from dividends, interest, royalties, and anything similar. We need not worry much about this here except to note that it does not include real estate income.

Under the old law, income was income and loss was loss. You could, thus, deduct any loss on real estate from your other income. Under the new law your personal income is considered active while your real estate loss is considered passive. Since you can't deduct a passive loss from active income, you can't, in general, write off real estate.

The Big Exclusion

The purpose of the 1986 Tax Reform Act was to prevent large investors in real estate from avoiding paying taxes with huge amounts of depreciation. However, the real estate industry raised a hue and cry, pointing out that there were numerous small investors for whom the loss was an essential element of investment. (On many properties without the write-off, there's no way to make a profit or even to break even.)

Hence, the government also passed an important exception to the above rule. This exception provides up to a $25,000 allowance for write-offs. In other words, you can continue to write off up to $25,000 in losses from real estate against your active income, provided you meet certain qualifications.

The qualifications aren't difficult to understand, but they are quite specific. There are only two of them:

Qualification 1—You Must Actively Participate in the Business of Renting the Property

This can be tricky, after all, what does "actively participate" really mean? Obviously if you own the property and are the only person directly involved in handling the rental—you advertise it, rent it, handle maintenance and clean up, collect the rent, etc.—you materially participate.

However, there are gray zones. Generally if you own less than 10 percent of the property, you probably don't qualify. Also, if you don't *personally* determine the rental terms, approve new tenants, sign for repairs, or approve capital improvements and the like, you also may not qualify.

The question always comes up, "What if I hire a management firm to handle the property for me?" This is even grayer. In general, a management firm is probably okay to use as long as you continue to materially participate (determine rental terms, approve new tenants, sign for repairs or capital improvements, and the like). If you are going to use a management firm (something this book does not recommend), be sure that you have your attorney check over the agreement you sign with the firm to see that it does not characterize you as not materially participating and thus prevent you from deducting any loss.

Qualification 2—Your Adjusted Gross Income Must Not Exceed $150,000

If it is below $100,000, you qualify for the entire $25,000 exception. If it is between $100,000 and $150,000, you lose 50 cents of the allowance for every dollar your income exceeds $100,000. Figure 13-1 will help explain this.

Since most small investors have incomes under $100,000, the allowance applies to them. If they materially participate in the property and their incomes stay low, they can continue to deduct their losses on real estate up to the $25,000 limitation. (However, with inflation, incomes will gradually rise until by the year 2000—if this law remains in effect—it will have much less benefit for most investors.)

Phasing Out $25,000 Allowance as Income Increases

Income	Allowance	Income	Allowance	Income	Allowance
$100,000	$25,000	117,000	16,500	134,000	8,000
101,000	24,500	118,000	16,000	135,000	7,500
102,000	24,000	119,000	15,500	136,000	7,000
103,000	23,500	120,000	15,000	137,000	6,500
104,000	23,000	121,000	14,500	138,000	6,000
105,000	22,500	122,000	14,000	139,000	5,500
106,000	22,000	123,000	13,500	140,000	5,000
107,000	21,500	124,000	13,000	141,000	4,500
108,000	21,000	125,000	12,500	142,000	4,000
109,000	20,500	126,000	12,000	143,000	3,500
110,000	20,000	127,000	11,500	144,000	3,000
111,000	19,500	128,000	11,000	145,000	2,500
112,000	19,000	129,000	10,500	146,000	2,000
113,000	18,500	130,000	10,000	147,000	1,500
114,000	18,000	131,000	9,500	148,000	1,000
115,000	17,500	132,000	9,000	149,000	500
116,000	17,000	133,000	8,500	150,000	0

Figure 13-1.

Understanding the Allowance

On the surface, the allowance and the qualifications may seem straight-forward. But, they can be tricky. For example, here are some other considerations:

1. The income used to determine whether you qualify is your *gross adjusted* income. This means your income after you have taken deductions such as some retirement plan contributions (not IRAs), alimony, moving expenses, and others. You may find that you really do have a small enough income to benefit from some or all of the allowance.
2. The allowance does not apply to farms. If you materially participate in the running of a farm, other rules apply—see your accountant or tax attorney.
3. Those who don't qualify for taking the deduction against their active income also cannot take the deduction against their portfolio income. (Remember, portfolio income came from interest, dividends, royalties, etc.)

Depreciation

As noted earlier, depreciation is an annual deduction taken against an asset. It is a way of capitalizing that asset over its useful life.

The tax law of 1986 substantially changed the rules on depreciation. It increased the term from under 20 to nearly 30 years and also decreased the rate at which depreciation could be taken. The rules for depreciation are quite complex and you should have an accountant or tax attorney set up the depreciation schedules for you when you do your taxes.

Sales

Thus far we've been talking about the tax advantages of rental real estate during the period of ownership. But what about when you sell? Are there any plusses then?

Basically as of this writing, gain on the sale of residential real estate is treated the same as personal income. There is no tax break. However, there is much confusion over this, so let's consider some of the errors that many people make:

Rollovers

The biggest error that most folks make when they sell residential real estate is to think that they can roll over their gains as long as they invest
the money within 2 years in a property of equal or greater value. I mention this up front because I can't count the number of times investors
have told me they planned to do this.

The rule on rollovers applies to your personal residence only. You don't roll
over investment property. (The rollover rules themselves are fairly complex, with qualifications for you and the house as well as specific time periods—check with your accountant and/or tax attorney.) If you have an
investment house that you have been renting, generally speaking you
can't roll it over.

Trades

You may, however, trade your property for another of "like kind" and
defer the gain to a future date. Tax-free trades are commonly done with
investment real estate and they may offer you a way of deferring taxes
while moving up or down to other properties. Keep in mind, however,
that this is one of the most complex areas of real estate taxation. Errors
made in the structuring of a trade can nullify the desired tax consequences. A tax-free trade should only be attempted under the guidance
of a skilled real estate tax and trade consultant. (There are trader groups
in most areas—check with your local real estate board.)

Capital Gains Taxes

I have heard otherwise reasonable people say, "At least when I sell my
property I won't have to worry about paying capital gains taxes." This
kind of talk is sheer craziness since capital gains tax is a *benefit*, not a
drawback.

Prior to 1986 there was a special capital gains rate that applied on the
sale of real estate. It was substantially lower than the rate for ordinary income taxes. However, when taxes were lowered in 1986, the capital gains
rate was eliminated. As of this writing, there is no capital gains tax rate.

Capital Gains Explained. Since a capital gains rate may be adopted
again in the near future (and dropped again as well), it's worthwhile to
say a few words about it.

Capital gains has been a much politicized issue with Republicans
claiming it's an incentive for investors and Democrats saying its a bail-
out for the rich. To my way of thinking, both positions have an element
of truth, but both also miss the big point. ·

Capital gains is just that, a tax on capital. When we study economics (at least capitalistic economics), we discover that capital is the essential ingredient for economic growth. The poor countries of Eastern Europe quickly found that out when they tried to move from a communistic to a capitalistic form of economy.

Capital is what allows us to borrow enough money (80 percent or more) to buy our rental house as well as to have money to put down. (The money we put down is *our* capital; the money we borrow is *someone else's* capital.) It's what allows a business to expand. In short, without capital, there is no growth. Therefore, does it make sense to tax capital? The more tax there is on capital, the less growth (because there's less capital). The less tax on capital, the more growth.

In some economic models (involving several European countries), there is no tax at all on a capital gain. For example, you invest $20,000 in a house and later sell for a profit of $100,000. In theory your capital gain is $80,000. (Forgetting for a moment about tax base, expenses, and the other means of calculating gain.) In these models if you now invest this $80,000 in other property (or a business or other capital investment), there is no tax. You are taxed only if you convert that $80,000 to personal income (i.e., you spend it on yourself in the form of living expenses, a new car, clothes, etc.).

It's easy to see that under the model described above, capital is encouraged to flow back into the system. Under our present taxation codes, however, capital reinvestment is discouraged. We tax capital gain just as we would ordinary income—we make no distinction. Hence, there's no disincentive to spending that capital on ourselves instead of reinvesting it.

I personally favor the above model—no tax of any kind on capital that is reinvested. However, since that is unlikely to come to pass, I favor the next best thing, a special capital gains tax rate. Under this rate, when you sell your property, you pay a lower tax rate than you would pay on your ordinary income from wages, commissions, etc. I suggest you give a little thought to the matter and come to your own conclusions. The capital gains issue is going to be before us for some time to come with frequent law changes likely to affect real estate both positively and adversely.

Installment Sales

Installment sales mean that when you sell, you don't get all of your money up front. Instead, you get a portion and the remainder is paid to you over a period of years. With regard to taxes, the question is do you pay tax at the time of the sale on the full amount of gain or do you pay as each installment is made?

Under the 1986 tax law, in general you will probably have to pay all or a significant portion of the gain at the time of the sale, although there are many, many extenuating circumstances. The law here is again extraordinarily complex and there are so many issues involved that each property has to be taken separately. This is an area that definitely needs the assistance of your tax counselor.

Suspended Losses

This is an area that is also relatively new. It refers to losses that you might incur on a rental property but can't take against your ordinary income because you don't qualify for the $25,000 allowance described earlier. What happens to those losses?

The answer is that you get them when you sell. For example, if you've had a $5,000 loss for 5 years on a rental house but couldn't take it as a write off against your income, you can take $25,000 when you sell.

The method the IRS requires for calculating the loss and then applying it at the time of sale is, once again, complex. Yet another area for your personal tax counselor.

The Bottom Line

There are not nearly as many tax advantages to owning real estate as there were only a few years ago—and there may be fewer still in the future. Congress and the President, faced with enormous budget deficits and limited income, have often chosen to "hit real estate on the head" rather than to simply raise taxes across the board, which appears to be politically unpalatable. You as a property owner, unfortunately, must pay the consequences.

Just a few years ago one of the big advantages of real estate was the ability to convert the tax on ordinary income to the lower capital gains rate. You could buy a property, hold it for an appropriate period of time, and then resell. At the time of the sale, the lower capital gains rates and not the higher ordinary income rates would apply. As we've seen, this advantage is gone. Other advantages may likewise be gone in the future. There is nothing to say that the government might not do away with the $25,000 allowance that permits deduction on real estate losses for lower income taxpayers. Or that tax-free trades might be disallowed.

Nevertheless, the fact remains that even without any tax incentives, real estate can be the hottest game in town. Bought at the bottom of a cold market and sold near the top of a hot one, I know of no other investment that compares in terms of potential profit.

14
Tracking the Turnaround

Recently I was teaching one of my sons to drive. He has subsequently progressed to become an excellent driver. However, back then, he was learning and he was hesitant to make a move into the flow of traffic on a busy street for fear of causing an accident.

If you've ever helped a son or daughter learn to drive, I'm sure you'll recall this situation. My son is driving, I'm in the passenger seat and we pull up to a moderately busy street. There's no traffic signal, only an arterial stop sign for us and cars are moving back and forth in front. I sit there waiting for him to pull into traffic. And sit and wait. And sit and wait. After about 5 minutes I suggest (cautiously, since he's already intimidated enough by the other cars), "Son, don't you think you ought to pull out?"

"I will, dad," he replies. "Just as soon as there's a break in the traffic." I look ahead. There's one car coming from the left, but it's maybe 600 feet away. Another is coming from the right, perhaps a quarter mile away. Both are moving no faster than 30 miles an hour. Meantime, I hear the honk of a car behind whose driver is getting impatient to move out. My son hears it, too, and he begins to get a wild, glazed look in his eye.

Best to wait, I tell myself. Don't make the boy any more nervous than he already is. Suddenly, with the closest approaching car no more than 50 feet off, the driver behind honks again and my son takes his foot off the break and stomps on the accelerator. We shoot across the road, me hanging onto the arm rest for dear life as he swerves to avoid the oncoming car, which now is also honking. In another moment he straightens out into the correct lane. "Pretty good, huh dad?" he says.

I wait for my heart to calm down a bit and reply, "Yup. Only next time, I think your mother ought to give you driving lessons."

What has this true story got to do with real estate? Nothing more than this. The entire strategy in this book has been to find the right property, rent it, and *hold* it. It's a good strategy, but it does have one potential problem. How do you know when it's the right time to give it the gas? Will you wait and wait when the market gets better and then only make your move when it's the wrong time? Or will you pull right out at the optimum time for cashing in? As with my son, timing here is very important. Only you want your timing to be better than his.

Learning about the Upturn

You'll know when the market finally gets hot once again. Everyone will be talking about it. All of a sudden houses will be rapidly selling once again. Your neighbors will tell you about the house up the street that sold for its asking price, almost unheard of. Brokers will call saying they have buyers for your property. And newspapers will be touting the reviving real estate market. There will be no lack of input when the market turns hot.

Only you may not want to wait until it's hot to get your money out. You may want to move sooner, when the market is just warming up. (Ideally, hanging on during the next upswing and then selling close to the top is the way to maximize your profits. However, picking the exact top can be tricky and you may be satisfied to sell for a handsome profit long before then.) The question becomes, how do you track the real estate market so you'll know what stage it's in? How do you know when its starting to turn, warming, and getting hot? That's what we'll examine in the rest of this chapter.

Tracking the Market Upward

A real estate upswing, historically, has a definite shape to it. It's an upswinging curve that gets steeper the further it goes, as shown in Figure 14-1.

Presumably when you read this, the market will be cold and you, as most people, will feel that real estate is pretty dead. Yes, you may be convinced that if you hold on it will eventually turn up. But you won't feel the excitement that comes from being involved in an up market.

In many ways it's the lack of excitement about real estate that keeps

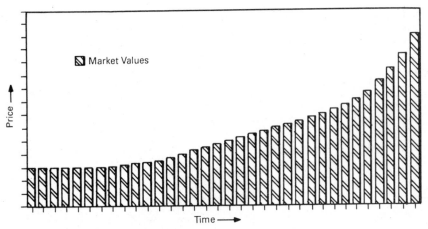

Figure 14-1 Illustration of a typical upswing.

the market cold—just as it's the excitement itself that pushes prices higher once conditions turn around. Let's look at the psychology of an up market.

At the Bottom

Once prices stabilize in a cold market and we hit the bottom, we tend to stay there for quite a while. Real estate is basically an illiquid commodity and it takes a lot of time, effort, and money to make it move. The bottom can last from 6 months to several years.

During this time certain things happen. As we've seen thus far in this book, those who *must* sell put their houses on the market and one way or another (either through sales or foreclosure) the properties change hands.

Those who can afford to hold either continue living in the properties or rent them out. However, as time passes even some of these begin putting their houses on the market and they too, one way or another, change hands.

In short, over time the existing inventory of houses is depleted. Eventually a day comes when buyers wake up and realize there aren't very many houses for sale. Suddenly buyers are competing against other buyers for a limited inventory.

List Price/Sales Price Ratio

You can tell when this happens by watching the ratio of list price to sales price. (This is another one of those helpful tools. As with the others, the information should be readily available from local brokers, particularly those who are computerized.) The list price is simply what the seller is asking for the property. The sales price is what a buyer actually pays for it. What you need is the average of all sales prices and all list prices, then compare the two.

In a cold market with a lot of buyers making low-ball offers, the difference between list and sales prices is often quite substantial, usually over 10 and sometimes over 20 percent.

However, as inventories shrink and buyers begin competing for homes, the ratio drops. If you were to plot this on a graph (not a bad thing to do if you have the time), you can actually see the ratio get smaller month by month as the market picks up.

Eventually the ratio will get very small, under 5 percent until in an extremely hot market it may actually go the other way, with sales prices exceeding list prices. (It doesn't happen often, but when it does, it has a special significance that we'll discuss shortly.)

Seller's Psychology

As prices begin to pick up, all those sellers who took their houses off the market reconsider. Would now be a good time to put them back on, they ask themselves? With prices starting to go up, one would naturally think the universal answer would be yes. And initially many sellers do put their homes back on the market, creating a false upswing which typically occurs off many bottoms.

But historically, the majority of would-be sellers don't actually put their houses up for sale. Many of them have decided to stay where they are instead of move. Others have found new jobs in the area and don't have to move. Still others have rented out their homes and have long-term leases and can't easily sell.

But behind all of this is a new psychology that begins to come into play. When sellers see prices of homes going up, they say to themselves, "Why should I sell now? If I just hang on for awhile, I can make even more money."

As a result, fewer houses than you might expect come onto the market as the price slowly begins to turn up. This, over time, starts producing an inventory shortage and, also over time, prices begin to climb higher and faster. (Keep in mind that we're talking about many months, even years for this to take place.)

In short, the higher that prices go, the less inclined sellers become to sell. It's the opposite of what happens in a declining market. As the price falls, more and more sellers try to sell to get yesterday's price. In a hot market fewer and fewer sellers try to sell, hoping to cash in on tomorrow's higher values.

One part of this psychology is forgetfulness. Usually by the time an up cycle happens, its been 4 or 5 years since the last down cycle and most of us have forgotten that prices can go both ways. Instead, we tend to sit back and count our paper profits.

This is when the curve changes from a flat bottom to a gentle upswing.

An Accelerating Market

News of the upswing is not kept quiet. Property owners joke with one another about how much their properties have gone up in value. Newspapers carry stories about the "healthy and robust" local real estate market. Brokers try to convince owners to list, telling them of the profits they can make.

All of this good news has one result—sellers tend to keep their homes off the market. Many would-be sellers become convinced that their homes are their greatest asset. Further, the longer they hold, the more their asset will be worth. (This was particularly true of sellers on the West Coast during the 1980s since real estate hadn't really gone down there— no sizeable loss in value—since the Second World War.)

As a result of a scarcity of resales, buyers competing for homes pay even more and prices begin to accelerate. Of course builders, seeing what's happening, jump on board and start new construction. But initially this has little effect because of the long delay involved in building. (Getting land, permits, environmental reports, building, and then selling can take anywhere from 18 months to 5 years.)

The Hot Market

We are now entering the last part of the curve, when it shoots upward. This is typically the shortest phase. Buyers become frantic in a very tight market. We begin seeing lines forming outside of new developments as buyers wait days to get a house. In the resale market, sellers often have offers from two or more buyers within hours of listing. Sometimes the offers are for more than the list price.

On and on it goes in a macabre dance with sellers laughing and patting themselves on the back at their good fortune and buyers paying more and more for fewer and fewer properties.

The Peak

One day a buyer wakes up and says, "This is ridiculous. Prices are crazy. I can't afford the down payment. I can't afford the monthly payments. I'd rather rent." Instead of buying, he or she pulls out of the market. Pretty soon another buyer does the same thing and yet another until suddenly, there's a shortage of buyers.

The market has just peaked. It doesn't take long for sellers to hear about this. Someone lists a house and it doesn't sell instantly. Instead it's for sale for 1 week, 2, a month—and it's offered at the same price as the one that sold in 2 hours down the street.

Sellers begin to think, "Maybe I'd better sell now while prices are still high."

Suddenly sellers from all over dump their houses on the market and the inventory swells. Suddenly those buyers who remain realize that they have a big pile to choose from. And they become choosy. They offer lower prices and lesser terms. And we're on the roller coaster ride down all over again.

Picking the Right Spot to Sell

If you bought during the last down turn, when should you sell? Should you sell as soon as the market turns up? Or should you wait until it gets really hot?

Tip

Sometimes the market doesn't get strong enough to warrant people waiting in line to get houses. Sometimes it only gets warm and then cools off, never getting hot. As a consequence, if you wait to see people lining up to get houses, you could wait too long. If your market never gets hot, you'll miss your chance to sell high.

The bottom line is that you should sell only when you feel you have made a big enough profit to justify your investment. It may be a 50 percent return, 100, or more or less. But when you're satisfied that your property has done well, sell.

If you're not at the peak, well, you'll just have to be satisfied with the profits you made. If you do sell at the top, you'll be able to congratulate yourself all the way to the bank. However, do keep in mind that if you can manage to sell before the peak and hang onto your profits, once the market turns down you can repeat the process all over again.

Tip

You can sometimes determine when the market peaks before anyone else. One way is to watch that ratio of sales prices to list prices. In a hot market it will be very small. But once it starts growing again, you'll know the market has turned down.

Another sign of a peaking market is lines of people waiting to buy. When people wait in line to get a new home (or there are multiple offers as soon as a resale is listed), you know you're getting close to the top. Soon (it may be 6 months or a year off) builders will be dumping new houses on the market. Soon buyers will be pulling up short, refusing to pay the stiff higher prices. Soon the market will be turning.

A Word of Consolation

What if you miss it!? What if the upturn is short lived and you don't take advantage of it? Remember, even if the market peaks and turns down before you sell, if you bought properly, you can always keep on renting. Ideally, you don't have to sell at all.

15

Conclusion: Getting Your Profits Out

The most obvious way to realize profits on real estate is to sell. Buy low and sell high was the motto with which we began. However, selling can itself be costly and there may be other alternatives. In this chapter, we'll look at the several ways that exist for getting your money out of your property.

Refinancing

First, let's consider refinancing. When we refinance, we get a newer and higher mortgage on the property and get cash back into our pockets.

Over the years some real estate gurus have advised comparing the ownership of rental property to owning an orchard. An orchard produces fruit and each year, you harvest that fruit. Instead of fruit, however, it's a new mortgage. When prices go up, you refinance and get your new equity out as cash. As quickly as the price goes up, you refinance, sometimes even doing it annually.

What these gurus failed to mention are two problems with this idea. First, higher mortgages mean higher payments. If you get a $50,000 increase in your mortgage value, you can be sure your monthly payments are likewise going to go up to service that mortgage, probably $500 a month or more.

Where's the money to come from to handle the increased debt? The

159

problem has always been that rental rates have not kept up with sales prices. Over the past 20 years rental rates in housing haven't even kept up with inflation. If you borrowed another $50,000 on your rental property, you'd have to take $500 a month out of your pocket to service that debt. Where is the advantage there?

Coming Rental Increases

Times are changing. New residential construction by the middle of 1990 was lower than at any time over the previous decade with the exception of the housing recession of 1982. This included construction not only of single-family houses but of apartments, condos, and other residential units as well. Put simply, it was a cold market and builders couldn't get construction loans to build or buyers to buy.

Reducing the number of new residential units coming onto the market will, eventually, help to raise prices. But in the short run it will have a different effect. It will act to raise rents.

The simple truth is that there are going to be fewer housing units available across the country during the middle of the 1990s. (This will undoubtedly result in an increase in building during the middle of the decade resulting in a surplus at the end, but that's a different story.)

There are going to be serious housing shortages. And as a result, landlords, for the first time in nearly a decade, should be able to significantly raise rents. Of course, rental increases will be kept down by rent restriction in many locales. However, rent restrictive laws usually apply only to multiple-family dwellings such as apartment buildings. Single-family homeowners in most cases are able to rent for what the market will bear.

As a result, for perhaps the first time in several decades what all those gurus have been saying about real estate being an orchard to be harvested may come true. If, over the course of 3 years, you can raise your rental rate $300 a month, you can afford a new mortgage for $30,000 more and not have to worry too much about making payments. For the first time in a long time, you may be able to truly have your cake and eat it—pull money out of the property and keep ownership. It could happen.

Refinancing Troubles

The second problem with refinancing that the gurus failed to mention, unfortunately, remains. It makes things difficult but not impossible.

Lenders starting in the mid-1980s began refusing to make first loans on equity for investors. Yes, if you were living in your house you could refinance your first mortgage and pull money out. However, if you owned a rental property, lenders would only loan you enough to pay off your existing mortgage and the costs involved in getting a new one. Where's the benefit there? (There actually is a benefit if you can refinance to a newer lower rate than your old existing mortgage.)

While refinancing by paying off your old loan and getting a new one remains a problem, refinancing by getting a second mortgage on rental property does not. You can get a second mortgage with ease on most rental real estate. Typically the rate may be 1 or 2 percent more in interest than for a first mortgage. Otherwise the loans are quite similar. (You may also have to pay around a half percent more than an owner-occupant would for a second.)

Many old-timers in real estate are sure to be saying, hold on there. Seconds are for short periods of time. The monthly cost of a second is likely to be far higher than that of a refinanced first.

Not necessarily. Many seconds these days are amortized (the repayment schedule) over 30 years, even though the payoff may be under 10 years. That makes their monthly payback quite competitive with first mortgages. In short if you get a second mortgage, you can often pull your money out with ease.

The bottom line is that today and even more so tomorrow as rental rates increase, the chances of getting your money out by refinancing look better and better.

Selling

Selling gets you out with your cash. Of course, there may be taxes to pay (see Chapter 13). And then there are the costs of selling. We're going to cover those briefly here so that you can make a fair judgment as to whether or not your property has appreciated sufficiently to warrant selling it.

Commission

You can expect to pay 5 to 7 percent, depending on the area of the country and the office with which you deal. On a $100,000 sale that's $5000 to $7000—a sizeable chunk of cash.

Is there any way to cut down on the commission? There really isn't if you use a broker and I always recommend using a broker as a means of getting an expedited sale. However, there are some avenues to sales open to investors that the average home owner really can't use.

For example, I have a friend who finds buyers in renters. He is always running one ad or another for rental houses that he has and he personally answers all the calls and talks to the potential tenants. Every so often he finds someone who is renting temporarily until they buy. He considers this a hot lead and follows up. He tries to convert this potential tenant into a potential buyer. He explains the benefits of the properties he has that he's currently trying to sell. He emphasizes that he has "bargains." And he points out that he will work with buyers on down payments and financing. To date he has sold seven properties this way without the use of an agent or without paying a commission. (*Note*: If you are inexperienced in real estate you should have the aid of a competent real estate attorney or professional to guide you through the technical aspects of a sale.)

Another alternative, though less likely to succeed in my experience, is to advertise your property in the "Income Property for Sale" section of your local newspaper. Investors often look here.

The trouble with this method is that the only people who read these ads are other investors and they are always looking strictly for bargains. Yes, you may find one who is willing to "take your property off your hands for you," but chances are you'll have to offer a lower than market price and better than market terms.

Finally there's the matter of selling to agents themselves. It doesn't hurt to become friends with as many agents as you can. They are always looking for rental properties to own. (Being in the business, it's easy for them to find tenants and manage properties.) Keep in mind, however, that agents typically don't have a lot of cash to put down and lenders don't like to loan to them.

This latter may need a bit more explanation. Lenders are well aware that real estate agents wheel and deal in order to make commissions. Even though the documentation presented to the lender may reflect a perfectly arms length deal, I have yet to find a lender who isn't prejudiced against agents. Usually they fear that somehow, some way, the agent is not putting in the full down payment or otherwise is conniving on the deal. This is not to say that agents can't get financing. It's just that it's much harder for them than for others.

Closing Costs

The closing costs are no different on a rental house than on an owner-occupied dwelling. They will typically be 1 to 3 percent of the sales price.

What is different is that if you're selling to another investor, sometimes you can avoid some of the normal costs. For example, I have sold rental property where the investor knew and trusted me. She obtained a preliminary title report which showed all the mortgages on the property and the other liens. Satisfied with this, she decided to move ahead. I simply transferred title to her in a deed which I drew up and which she recorded and she assumed the FHA loan I had on the property. We had no escrow, no title insurance, virtually no fees at all.

This isn't for everyone and does run some risks. (An escrow is normally advisable since it assures that you get your money and the buyer gets clear title. Most buyers also will insist on title insurance to protect their interest.) However, if you get a cooperative buyer, it can save you both a bundle.

The Bottom, Bottom Line

Buy, rent, and hold—then refinance or sell. In this book we've examined the strategy and the application. What remains is the doing.

There is one other point. When you go out there and begin looking for investment property and start renting it, you'll find you're not working in a vacuum. There will be others doing the same thing you are.

Yes, they are competitors. But if you work with them, they can often clue you in on all sorts of good deals that you might otherwise miss. If there's one last tip I can impart, it's this (it's also probably the most important).

Tip

Work with everyone and be a straight shooter. When push comes to shove, your reputation, the extent and quality of it, can be more important than money itself in getting you a good deal.

Index

About the Author

Robert Irwin has been a successful real estate broker for 25 years and has steered countless buyers and sellers through every kind of real estate transaction imaginable. He has been a consultant to lenders, brokers, and investors, and is actively involved in buying and selling residential real estate for profit. He is one of the most knowledgeable and prolific authors in the field of real estate, with such books to his credit as *Making Mortgages Work for You, How to Find Hidden Real Estate Bargains, How to Find and Manage Profitable Properties, Tips and Traps When Buying a Home,* and *Tips and Traps When Selling a Home.*